Microsoft Internet Explorer 5

fast & easy ™

Send Us Your Comments

To comment on this book or any other PRIMA TECH title, visit PRIMA TECH's reader response page on the Web at **www.prima-tech.com/comments**.

How to Order:

For information on quantity discounts, contact the publisher: Prima Publishing, P.O. Box 1260BK, Rocklin, CA 95677-1260; (916) 632-4400. On your letterhead, include information concerning the intended use of the books and the number of books you wish to purchase. For individual orders, visit PRIMA TECH's Web site at **www.prima-tech.com**.

Microsoft® Internet Explorer 5

fast & easy™

Coletta Witherspoon

PRIMA
TECH

A Division of Prima Publishing

A Division of Prima Publishing

Prima Publishing and colophon, PRIMA TECH, and Fast & Easy are trademarks or registered trademarks of Prima Communications, Inc., Rocklin, California 95677.

Publisher: Matthew H. Carleson

Associate Publisher: Nancy Stevenson

Managing Editor: Dan J. Foster

Senior Acquisitions Editor: Deborah F. Abshier

Project Editor: Kevin W. Ferns

Technical Reviewer: Ray Link

Copy Editor: Maria Paddock

Interior Layout: Shawn Morningstar

Cover Design: Prima Design Team

Indexer: Katherine Stimson

Microsoft, Windows, Windows NT, Outlook, MSN, and FrontPage are trademarks or registered trademarks of Microsoft Corporation.

Important: If you have problems installing or running Microsoft Internet Explorer 5, go to Microsoft's Web site at **www.microsoft.com**. Prima Publishing cannot provide software support.

Prima Publishing and the author have attempted throughout this book to distinguish proprietary trademarks from descriptive terms by following the capitalization style used by the manufacturer.

Information contained in this book has been obtained by Prima Publishing from sources believed to be reliable. However, because of the possibility of human or mechanical error by our sources, Prima Publishing, or others, the Publisher does not guarantee the accuracy, adequacy, or completeness of any information and is not responsible for any errors or omissions or the results obtained from the use of such information. Readers should be particularly aware of the fact that the Internet is an ever-changing entity. Some facts may have changed since this book went to press.

ISBN: 0-7615-1742-1

Library of Congress Catalog Card Number: 98-67162

Printed in the United States of America

99 00 01 02 03 HH 10 9 8 7 6 5 4 3 2 1

To Paula Amelsberg

Acknowledgments

I can still remember my first online experience, way back in the early 90s. I was amazed at the amount of information I could find. It was like having the world's largest library in my very own living room, and I was addicted. What is so incredible about the Internet is the number of opportunities that it has created. The ease with which one can communicate with people from all over the world has led to building new personal, professional, and business relationships. My hope is that this book will help you understand the tools of the Internet and gain confidence exploring this fascinating world. May you find a path to a better life during your journey.

I want to thank everyone at Prima for all their hard work and great support. It's always a pleasure working with Debbie Abshier and Kevin Ferns. Maria Paddock and Ray Link did a great job looking over the manuscript. Thanks for your input, help, and corrections!

About the Author

Coletta Witherspoon is a confirmed Web junkie. She was introduced to computers in the late 70s and began working as a technical writer in the environs of Redmond in the mid 80s. After a decade of suits and ties, she and her husband moved to a small farm in the middle of nowhere, converted the living room into an office, and now conduct all their business over the Internet. Coletta is the author of several *Fast & Easy* series books from PRIMA TECH.

Contents
at a Glance

Contents

PART IV
MANAGING MAIL AND NEWS
WITH OUTLOOK EXPRESS 129

Introduction

This *Fast & Easy* series guide from PRIMA TECH will help you quickly learn to use Internet Explorer 5.0 and its suite of Internet software tools. Internet Explorer and its components are designed to provide you with all of the tools necessary for you to take full advantage of what the World Wide Web offers. The complete package of Internet tools includes a Web browser, an integrated e-mail program and newsreader, chat and videoconferencing tools, a Web page design program, and a plethora of multimedia devices.

The enormity of the World Wide Web and the sheer number of Internet Explorer components may seem overwhelming. This book will help you untangle the Web and show you how easy it is to use each Internet Explorer component. This *Fast & Easy* guide teaches you in a step-by-easy-step fashion, using clear language and illustrations that lead you through what you will see on your screen. You'll be comfortably surfing the Web in no time.

WHO SHOULD READ THIS BOOK?

As you thumb through this book, you may think that it is just for beginners because of the easy-to-follow directions and generous use of illustrations. But it is also the perfect tool for those who are familiar with the Internet and with Web browsing and who want to get up to speed with Internet Explorer 5.0 quickly. You may need to read all of the individual chapters in a particular section of the book to master its subject matter, or you may only need to read certain chapters to fill in the gaps in your existing knowledge. This book is structured to support the method that suits you best.

This book also makes a great reference tool. With all of the software available today and the myriad software programs that you may use in your personal and business life, sometimes you just need a quick reminder of how to use a program to perform different tasks. You can easily look up a task without having to wade through pages of descriptions, definitions, and reference material.

HELPFUL HINTS TO INCREASE YOUR SKILLS

The use of step-by-step instructions and detailed illustrations helps you learn quickly. Explanations are kept to a minimum to help speed your progress. Included in this book are additional elements that will provide you with more information on how to work with the Internet Explorer components without encumbering your progress:

✦ **Tips** often offer shortcuts for various Internet Explorer features, which make your job a little easier and add some adventure to your Web travels.

✦ **Notes** offer additional information about a feature or advice on how to use the feature while you are Web surfing.

Also, the appendix shows you how to get Internet Explorer 5.0 from Microsoft's Web site. You'll learn how to install the Internet Explorer browser and other add-on components on your computer.

Have fun with this *Fast & Easy* guide. It's the quickest and simplest way to learn Internet Explorer 5.0.

Aloha and happy surfing!

PART I
Getting Internet Explorer Up and Running

1 Starting and Exiting Programs

Internet Explorer can be installed with a number of components that are part of the Internet Explorer suite. As with other software suites, Internet Explorer components can be used separately or in conjunction with each other. Although there are several components to learn, this does not have to be an overwhelming task. The components in the Internet Explorer suite share a number of common elements, which gives you a familiar place to start with each new component. In this chapter, you'll learn how to:

✦ Start Internet Explorer components

✦ Navigate elements common to all Internet Explorer components

✦ Exit Internet Explorer components

STARTING EXPLORER PROGRAMS

There are several methods for opening the various Internet Explorer components. This section shows you how to start programs using two easy methods.

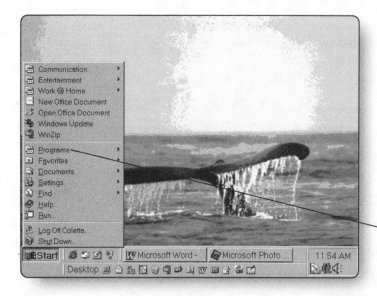

Beginning from the Start Menu

The most common way to open any Windows program is to use the Start button.

1. **Click** on the **Start button** on the Windows taskbar. The Start Menu will appear.

2. **Move** the **mouse pointer** to Programs. The Programs menu will appear.

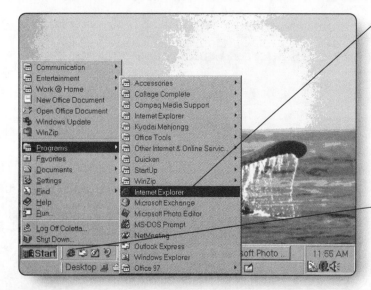

3. **Click** on **Internet Explorer**. The program will open.

NOTE

You can also open Internet Explorer by clicking on the Internet Explorer icon on the Quick Launch toolbar.

USING INTERNET EXPLORER COMPONENTS

When you look at the screens for various Internet Explorer components, you may think that you'll never understand how all these programs work. Don't be discouraged. All of the Internet Explorer components use the same familiar interface.

Using Toolbars

The toolbars in the Internet Explorer components contain a number of buttons. These buttons can be thought of as shortcuts to the more commonly used menu commands.

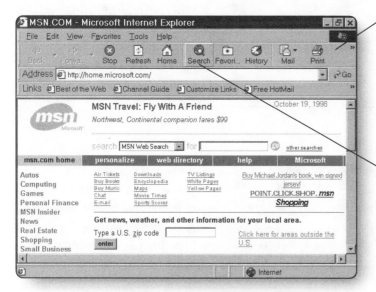

1. Place the **mouse pointer** over a button on the toolbar. The button will be highlighted. If you've turned off the text labels, a tool tip will appear telling you what function the button performs.

2. Click on the **Search button**. The command associated with the button will be executed. In this example, the Search pane displays. You can access several Search engines from this pane that can help you find information on any subject that interests you.

TIP

Click on the Search button a second time. The Search pane will close.

Executing Menu Commands

Menus contain all of the functions that a program can perform. Each program contains several menus, each of which offers a number of related commands.

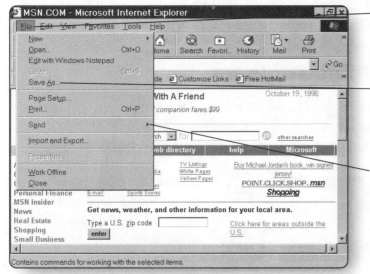

1. **Click** on a **menu bar** on the toolbar to **open** a **menu**. A drop-down list will appear.

✦ When a menu command is followed by an ellipsis (...), a dialog box will appear if that command is selected.

✦ When a right-pointing arrowhead follows a menu command, another menu will appear when the mouse pointer is moved over the command.

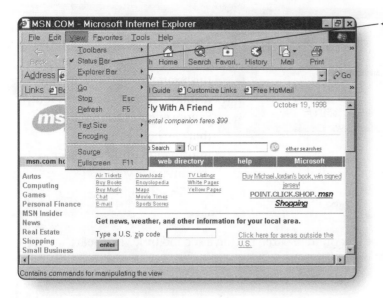

✦ If a menu command is preceded by a check box, that command acts as a toggle. A check mark turns the function on; a missing check mark means the function is turned off.

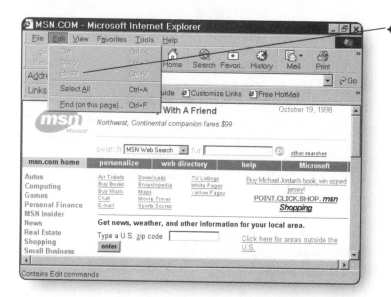

✦ When a menu command is grayed out, it means the command is not available. You may need to perform some preliminary action before you can use the grayed-out command.

Finding Shortcut Menus with a Right-Click

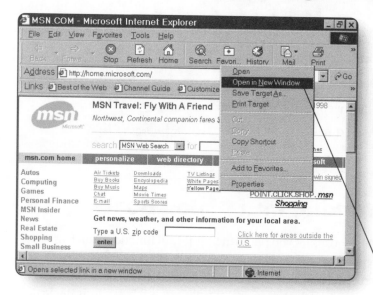

If you're looking for another means of executing commands, try using the right-click method. When you right-click on any element inside a component window, a menu will appear. This menu contains all of the commands that can be executed for the element you selected.

1. **Right-click** on the **object**. A menu will appear.

2. **Click** on a **command**. The command will be executed.

Using Command Shortcuts

You may have noticed the keyboard shortcuts listed on the right side of some menus. You can use these shortcuts to open menus without clicking on them. As you become familiar with the Internet Explorer components, you may want to rely on these keyboard shortcuts to increase your productivity and to help decrease wrist strain caused by excessive mouse usage. The following table lists a few of the more common keyboard shortcuts that you may want to memorize:

TO EXECUTE THIS COMMAND	DO THIS
Use Help	Press the F1 key
Refresh the contents of a window	Press the F5 key
Stop downloading	Press the Esc key
Open a file	Press the Ctrl and O keys simultaneously (Ctrl+O)
Print a file	Press Ctrl+P
Find something on a page	Press Ctrl+F
Delete selected text	Press Ctrl+X
Make a copy of the selected text	Press Ctrl+C
Paste the copied text	Press Ctrl+V

Working with Dialog Boxes

Dialog boxes let you perform a variety of functions, such as saving files and setting preferences. Dialog boxes contain elements such as tabs that group several dialog boxes into one, buttons that display secondary dialog boxes, and drop-down lists that let you select a number of predefined options.

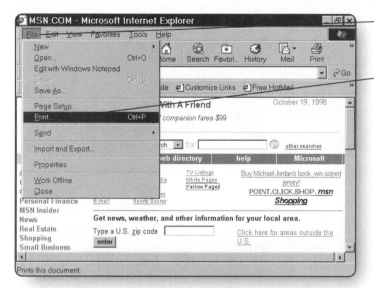

1. Click on **File**. The File menu will appear.

2. Click on **Print**. The Print dialog box will open.

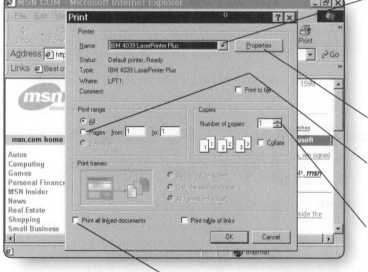

✦ Open drop-down lists by clicking on the down arrow within the dialog box to display the list of options; then click on the option you want to choose.

✦ Access a secondary dialog box by clicking on a button.

✦ Select one of a group of options by clicking on the option button.

✦ Adjust numbers by clicking on the up arrow or the down arrow.

✦ Turn features on and off by clicking on the check box next to the feature name.

3. Click on **OK**. The command will be executed.

TIP

If you want to close a dialog box without accepting any of the changes you have made, click on the Cancel button.

Moving around with Scroll Bars

You will find two types of scroll bars in Internet Explorer components: vertical scroll bars and horizontal scroll bars.

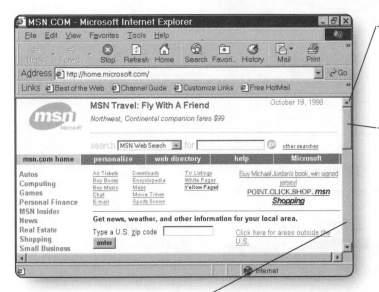

✦ Click on the arrow at either end of the vertical or horizontal scroll bar. This will move you through the document line-by-line.

✦ Place the mouse pointer over the box located in the scroll bar. Press and hold the mouse button and drag the box. Release the mouse button when you reach the desired place in the document. This allows you to move to any point in the document.

✦ Click the mouse button inside the scroll bar to view the document one screen at a time.

Resizing Frames

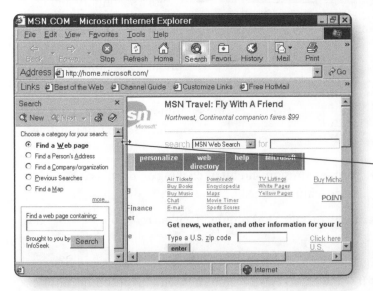

Some component windows are divided into several frames. These frames can be resized so that you can see more or less of the content within them.

1. Click and hold the mouse button on the border between the frames. The mouse pointer will change to a double arrow.

2. Drag the mouse pointer in either direction. The frames will change size.

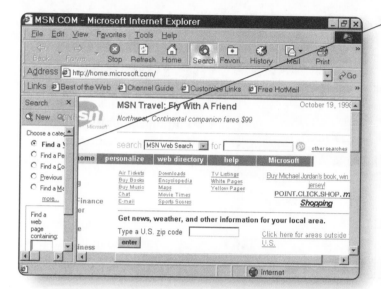

3. Release the **mouse button** when the frames are the desired size.

EXITING INTERNET EXPLORER PROGRAMS

As is the case with all Windows programs, you have several options for closing Internet Explorer components.

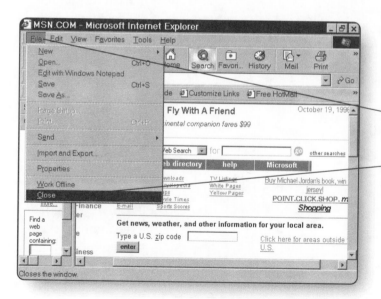

Exiting a Program from the File Menu

1. Click on **File**. The File menu will appear.

2. Click on **Close**. The program will close.

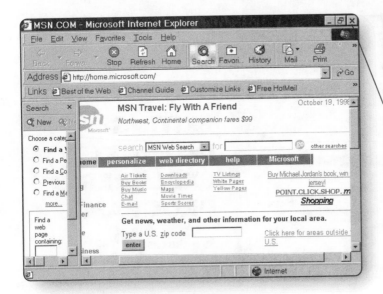

Exiting a Program from the Title Bar

1. **Click** on the **Close button** ([×]) in the upper right corner of the program window. The program will close.

2 Getting Help

After reading this book, you will feel comfortable using the Internet Explorer programs. But this is just the beginning of your journey. As you get more involved in the Internet, you'll find new uses for the Internet Explorer programs and discover features that you'll want to explore. There are lots of places to turn to for assistance. In this chapter, you'll learn how to:

✦ Get help using the Help button

✦ Get help using the Help topics

✦ Get help from Microsoft's Web site

GETTING HELP USING THE HELP BUTTON

As you work in a program, you'll notice the question mark (?) button at the top right corner of various dialog boxes. If you are unsure of what function different options perform, use the Help button for quick answers.

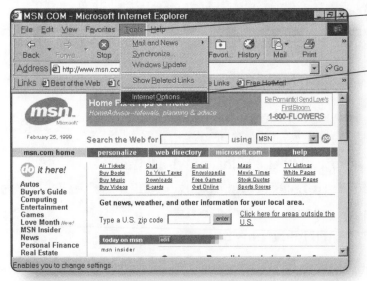

1. **Click** on **Tools**. The Tools menu will appear.

2. **Click** on **Internet Options**. The Internet Options dialog box will appear with the General tab displayed.

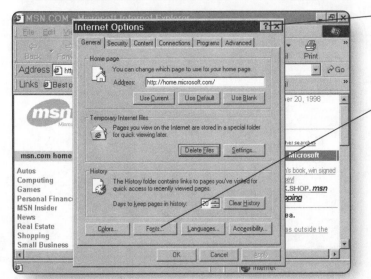

3. **Click** on the **Help button**. The mouse pointer will change to a pointer with a question mark.

4. **Click** on the **item** about which you want more information. A screen tip will appear.

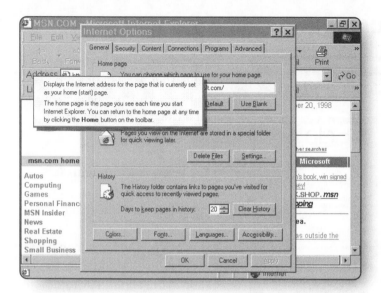

5. Click **anywhere** outside of the screen tip. The screen tip will disappear and you can continue working with the program.

SEARCHING THE HELP FILE

If the Help button doesn't answer your questions, it's time to go to the Help topics and search for an answer.

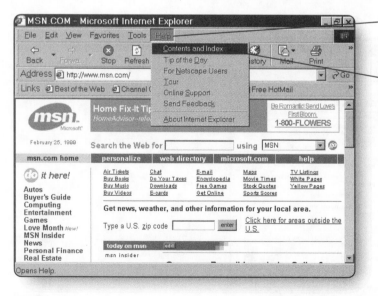

1. Click on **Help**. The Help menu will appear.

2. Click on **Contents and Index**. The Help topics dialog box will open.

Using the Contents Tab

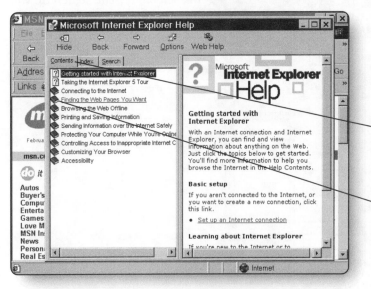

The Contents tab reads somewhat like a book's table of contents. You may have to hunt for a while to find the answer you need.

1. Click on the **Contents tab**. The list of topics will appear in the left frame of the dialog box.

2. Click on the **book icon** next to the topic that you want to know more about. The topic will expand to show the contents.

TIP

You can use the Back and Forward buttons to navigate between Help topics that you've already viewed.

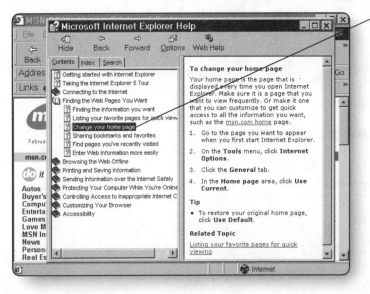

3. Click on the **item** with which you need help. The help topic will appear in the right frame.

Using the Index Tab

The Index dialog box looks something like the index that you find in the back of a book. You can either scroll through the list to find the topic you are looking for or you can type some keywords to reduce your search time.

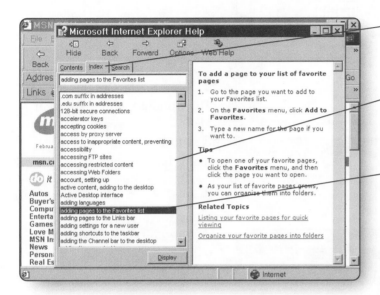

1. Click on the **Index tab**. The list of Help topics will appear in the left frame of the dialog box.

2. **Scroll through** the **list** of topics to find the topic with which you need help.

3. **Double-click** on the **topic**. The help file for the topic will appear in the right frame.

NOTE

You can also click on the topic to select it, then click on the Display button to display the Help file.

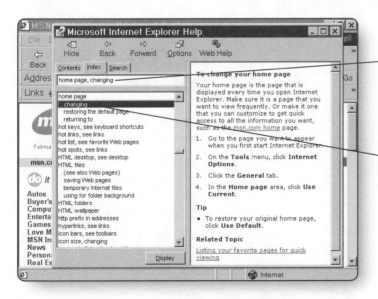

4. **Type keywords** in the text box for the subject on which you need help. The closest match will display in the list of topics.

5. **Double-click** on the **topic** that is the closest match. The Help topic for that item will appear in the right frame.

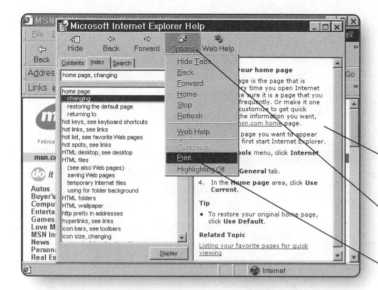

Printing Help Files

If you want to keep a paper copy of a help file, you can use the Help print function.

1. **Display** the **Help file** that you want to print.

2. **Click** on the **Options button**. The Options menu will appear.

3. **Click** on **Print**. The Print dialog box will appear.

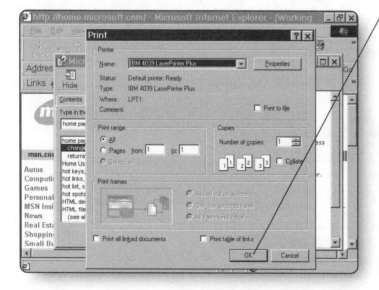

4. **Click** on **OK**. The Help topic will be printed for you.

GETTING HELP ON THE WEB

Microsoft provides a wealth of information on its Web site. If the program Help files haven't answered your questions, it's time to get online and give Microsoft a call. Before you try to get online help, make sure you are connected to your Internet Service Provider (ISP).

Accessing the Online Web Tutorial

If you're looking for a quick tutorial on how the Internet works, take the Online Tutorial. This option is only found in the Internet Explorer browser.

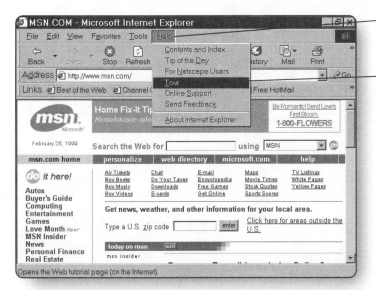

1. Click on **Help**. The Help menu will appear.

2. **Click** on **Tour**. The Welcome to the Internet Explorer 5 Tour home page will appear in the browser window.

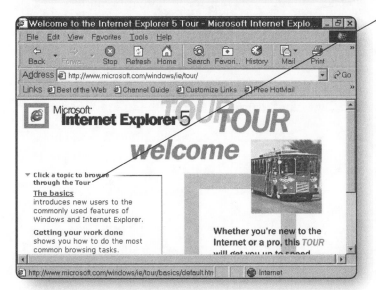

3. **Click** on a **hyperlink** that pertains to a subject that interests you. The corresponding Web page will appear.

NOTE

Hyperlinks are words or images that connect you to another Web page. Text hyperlinks are shown as underlined words on a Web page. When you place the mouse pointer over a hyperlink, the pointer will turn into a hand.

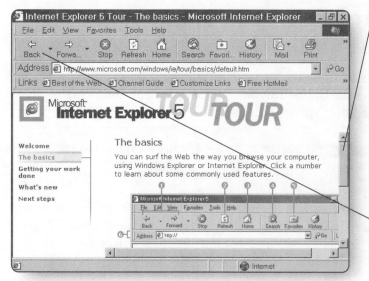

4. Use the **scroll bar** to scroll through the Web page as you read, until you come to the end of the page.

5. **Click** on the **Back button**. You will be returned to the Internet Explorer 5 Tour home page.

OTHER HELPFUL WEB SITES

If you're looking for a few good sites to help you learn more about the Internet, check these out:

Internet 101: An Ideal Place for Beginners to Start at http://www2.famvid.com/i101/internet101.html

Learn the Net: An Internet Guide and Tutorial at http://www.learnthenet.com/english/index.html

Smart Surfing home page at http://www.smartsurfing.mci.com/

Finding Online Help

The Microsoft online technical support Web pages offer a wealth of information about all of Microsoft's products.

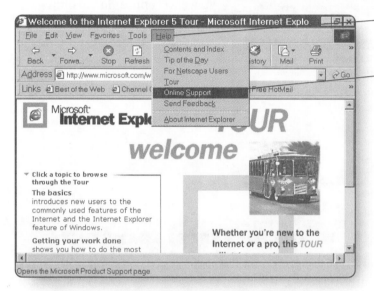

1. **Click** on **Help**. The Help menu will appear.

2. **Click** on **Online Support**. The Microsoft Personal Support Center home page will appear.

NOTE

In Outlook Express, the Online Support command can be found under the command called Microsoft on the Web.

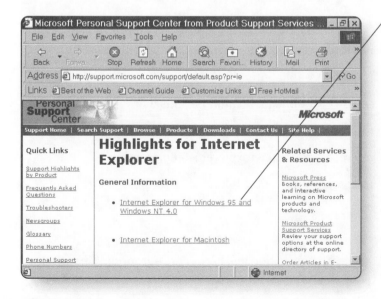

3. **Click** on the **Internet Explorer hyperlink** that corresponds to your computer operating system. The Support Highlights page will appear.

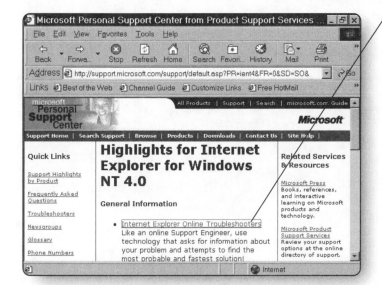

4. **Scroll** through the **page** and **click** on the **hyperlink** that seems most likely to answer your questions. The selected Web page will appear in the browser window.

WHERE THE EXPERTS HANG OUT

Here are a few newsgroups where you can ask questions and hopefully find a few answers:

comp.infosystems.www.browsers.ms-windows

microsoft.public.inetexplorer.ie5.browser

microsoft.public.inetexplorer.ie5.outlookexpress

microsoft.public.internet.mail

microsoft.public.internet.mschat

microsoft.public.inetexplorer.ie5.mschat

microsoft.public.internet.netmeeting

microsoft.public.inetexplorer.ie5.netmeeting

microsoft.public.inetexplorer.ie5.frontpad

NOTE

You'll learn how to find and access newsgroups in Chapter 13, "Using News."

PART I REVIEW QUESTIONS

1. What are the different ways that you can open Internet Explorer components? *See "Starting Explorer Programs" in Chapter 1.*

2. What happens when you click on the down arrow next to a toolbar button? *See "Exploring Common Elements in Internet Explorer Components" in Chapter 1.*

3. What does an ellipsis next to a menu command mean? *See "Exploring Common Elements in Internet Explorer Components" in Chapter 1.*

4. What happens when you right-click on a Web page element? *See "Exploring Common Elements in Internet Explorer Components" in Chapter 1.*

5. How do you exit Internet Explorer components? *See "Exiting Internet Explorer Programs" in Chapter 1.*

6. Where is the Help button located and what function does it perform? *See "Getting Help Using the Help Button" in Chapter 2.*

7. What are the two different ways you can use the Help Topics to find answers to your questions? *See "Searching the Help File" in Chapter 2.*

8. Can you print Help files? *See "Searching the Help File" in Chapter 2.*

9. Is it possible to find help using the Internet Explorer components on the Internet? *See "Getting Help on the Web" in Chapter 2.*

10. Which newsgroups offer help with using Internet Explorer components? *See "Getting Help on the Web" in Chapter 2.*

PART II

Learning to Use the Internet Explorer Browser

3 Navigating the Web

Are you ready to enter the World Wide Web? The Web is a collection of sites that contain an assortment of pages, pictures, sound effects, animations, and often some useful information. Everything on the Web is connected by hyperlinks. Think of hyperlinks as the hallways between Web sites, but instead of walking from site to site, you merely click on a hyperlink. In this chapter, you'll learn how to:

+ Use the Address bar

+ Navigate from one Web page to another

+ Keep track of page status with the Status Bar

STARTING FROM THE ADDRESS BAR

Begin by typing a Web address, or Uniform Resource Locator (URL), into the address bar. You may know of different addresses that you'd like to try, or if not, try the Prima home page (www.prima-tech.com).

NOTE

Before you start working with the Internet Explorer browser, you'll need to be connected to the Internet through your ISP. Your ISP should have provided you with instructions for creating a Dial Up Networking connection that you'll use to connect to their service.

Typing URLs

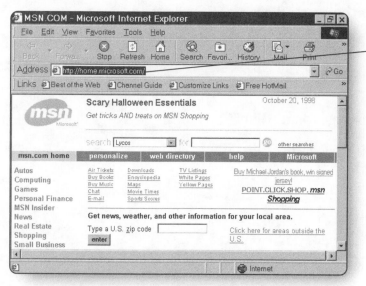

1. Click in the **Address bar**. The URL (Uniform Resource Locator) that is currently in the Address bar will be selected.

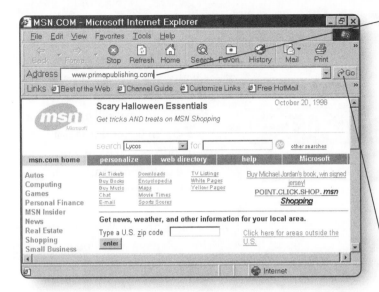

2. Type the **URL** of the Web page you want to visit. The first URL will disappear and the URL you are typing will display.

NOTE

You don't need to type the http:// part of the address. Internet Explorer will take care of that part for you.

3. Press the **Go button** when you are finished typing the URL. The Web page will appear in the browser window.

NOTE

The amount of time it takes to completely display the page will depend on your modem speed, Internet traffic, and the amount of content contained on the page.

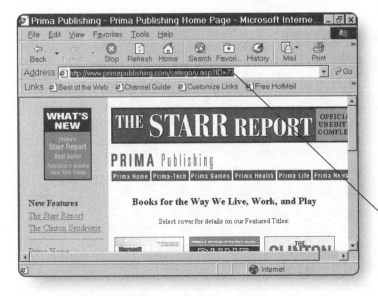

Using AutoComplete to Enter a URL

If you've typed Web addresses previously in the Address bar, Internet Explorer will attempt to guess which Web address you want.

1. Click in the **Address bar**. The URL presently in the Address bar will be highlighted.

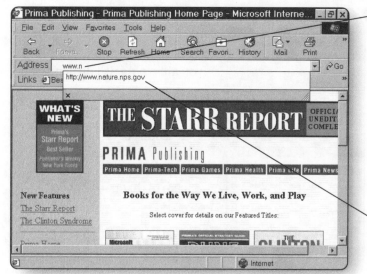

2. Begin typing the **Web address** of a Web page that you visited before. Internet Explorer will attempt to complete the address; the assumed portion of the Web address will appear in a drop-down list. If this is not the Web address you want, continue typing until the correct Web address appears.

3. Click on the **Web address**. The Web page will appear in the browser window.

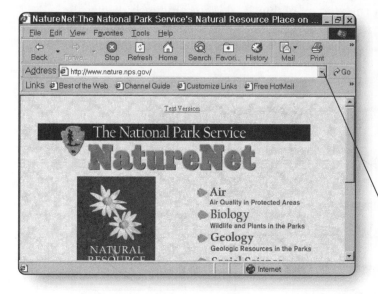

Accessing URLs from the Drop-Down List

The following is another shortcut that you can use to access Web addresses that you've visited before.

1. Click on the **down arrow** to the right of the Address bar. A list of URLs that you previously typed into the Address bar will appear.

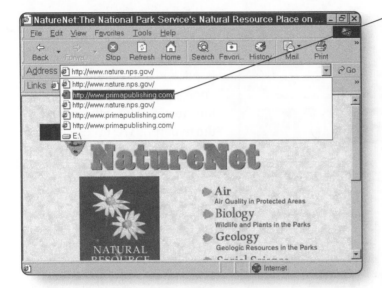

2. Click on a URL. The associated Web page will appear.

NAVIGATING BETWEEN WEB PAGES

Now you may want to try your hand at Web surfing. Web surfing is accomplished by clicking hyperlinks found on Web pages and letting the Web take you where it will. Hyperlinks can be words or images that connect one Web page to another. Text hyperlinks are the underlined words that you see on a Web page. Image hyperlinks may or may not have a border around them. It's easy to find a hyperlink: just move the mouse pointer around on a Web page until the pointer turns into a hand.

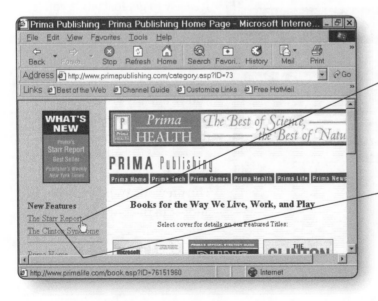

Clicking through Hyperlinks

1. Place the mouse pointer over a text hyperlink. The mouse pointer changes to a hand and the associated URL appears in the Status bar.

2. Click on the hyperlink. The linked Web page will appear in the browser window.

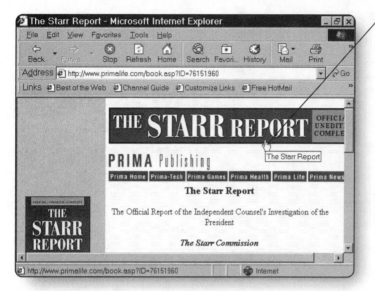

3. Place the **mouse pointer** over an image hyperlink. The mouse pointer changes to a hand, and a screen tip may appear that gives you some information about the page the hyperlink will access.

4. Click on the **hyperlink**. The linked Web page will appear in the browser window.

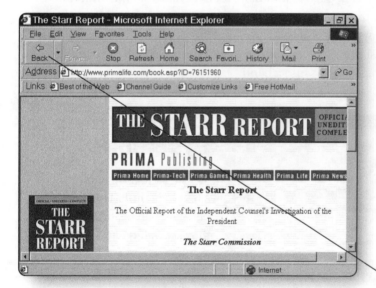

Using the Back and Forward Buttons

It's easy to get lost while you're surfing the Web, especially if you've been immersed for an hour or two. If you find that you want to look at Web pages you've already visited, use the Back and Forward buttons on the Internet Explorer toolbar.

1. Click on the **Back button**. The previous Web page will appear in the browser window.

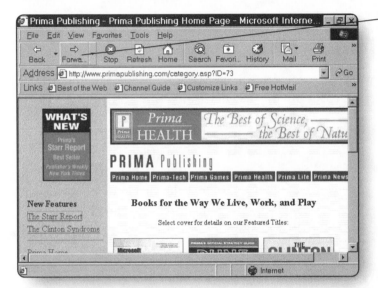

2. Click on the **Forward button**. You will be returned to the original page.

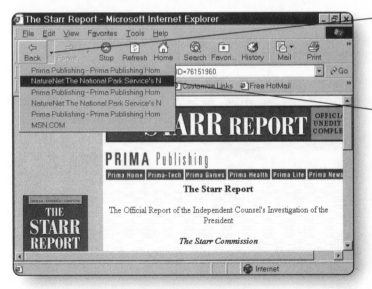

3. Click on the **down arrow** to the right of the Back button. A list of Web pages that you visited earlier will appear.

4. Click on a **Web page**. The Web page will appear in the browser window.

TIP

The down arrow to the right of the Forward button works the same way.

Looking at the Recent History List

If you want to view one of the last seven Web pages that you visited, check out the Recent History list.

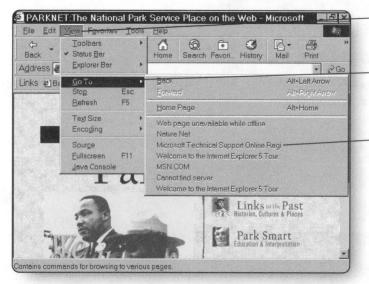

1. Click on **View**. The View menu will appear.

2. Click on **Go To**. A drop-down menu will appear.

3. Click on an **item** in the Recent History list. The Web page will appear in the browser window.

USING THE STATUS BAR

Along the bottom of the Internet Explorer browser window, you'll find the Status bar. The Status bar contains information to help you decide if you should click on a hyperlink, continue downloading a Web page, or enter sensitive information.

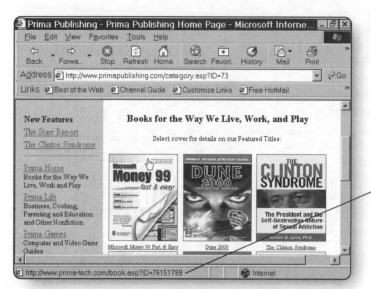

✦ When you hold the mouse pointer over a hyperlink, the URL address of the Web page to which you will be taken appears in the far left of the Status bar.

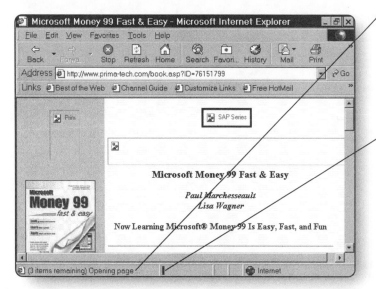

✦ When you click on a hyperlink and the linked page begins appearing in the browser window, the Status bar tells you how much of the page is left to download.

✦ The Status bar also shows you how the download is progressing.

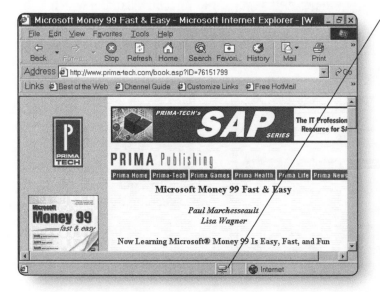

✦ If you view Web pages that are stored on your computer's hard drive when you're not connected to the Internet, the Work Offline icon appears in the Status bar.

TIP

You'll learn more about viewing Web pages offline in Chapter 7, "Working with Favorites."

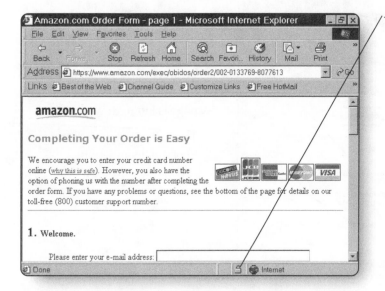

✦ When you have accessed a secure Web site where you can purchase products with your credit card, a Padlock icon will appear in the Status bar. Secure Web sites use encryption technologies to make sure that no one can eavesdrop on your Internet transmission and steal your credit card number.

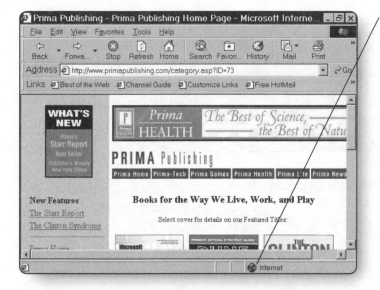

✦ You can tell under which Security Zone a Web page is categorized by looking at the Security Zone box located at the right side of the Status bar.

TIP

You'll learn more about Security Zones in Chapter 8, "Keeping Your Computer Safe."

4 Customizing the Browser

When you first open the Internet Explorer browser, you may find that the appearance of the toolbar, the font size, or the default home page is not to your liking. Well, don't despair; you can remodel the browser to suit your own taste. In this chapter, you'll learn how to:

✦ Choose a different home page

✦ Manipulate the toolbars

✦ Change the size of the text in Web pages

✦ Use the History list effectively

SETTING YOUR HOME PAGE

The home page is the first Web page you see when you open the Internet Explorer browser. The first time you use Internet Explorer, you may see a home page set for you by Microsoft, the computer manufacturer, or your ISP. You don't have to keep this home page; you can change it to something that is more useful or interesting to you.

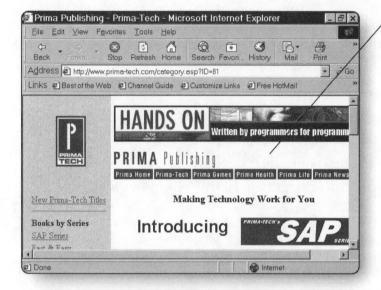

1. Open the **Web page** that you want to use as a home page.

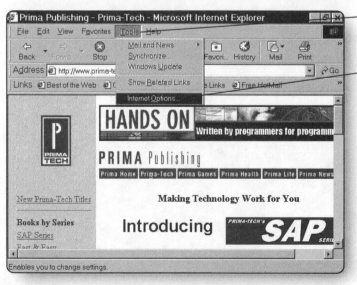

2. Click on **Tools**. The Tools menu will appear.

3. Click on **Internet Options**. The Internet Options dialog box will appear and the General tab will be on top.

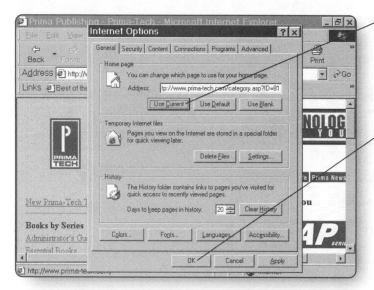

4. Click on the **Use Current button**. A URL will appear in the Address text box. This is the address for the page that will display in the browser window.

5. Click on **OK**. The next time you open Internet Explorer, this page will appear in the browser window.

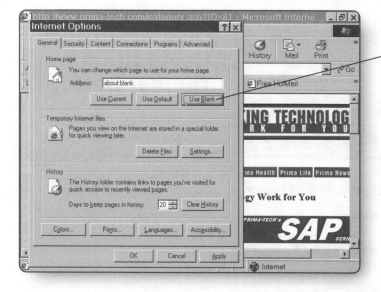

NOTE

If you want Internet Explorer to load quickly each time you open the browser, click on the Use Blank button. Your home page will open as a blank window.

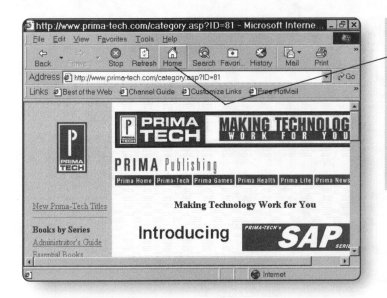

TIP

When you're cruising around the Internet, you can return to your home page easily with just a click of the Home button. Your default home page will appear in the browser window.

WORKING WITH TOOLBARS

You'll find that you spend a lot of time working with the various toolbars, so it's a good idea to learn how these toolbars work and set them up properly.

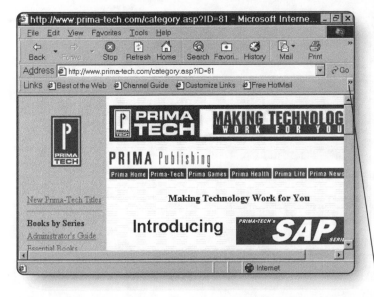

Displaying and Using Hidden Toolbar Buttons

If you're using a low screen resolution (such as 640 x 480), have a small monitor, or if you use a minimized browser window, you'll notice that not all of the toolbar buttons appear onscreen. However, it's easy to display and use the toolbar buttons that don't appear.

1. Click on the **double arrow** at the end of the Links toolbar. A menu appears that shows the hidden toolbar buttons.

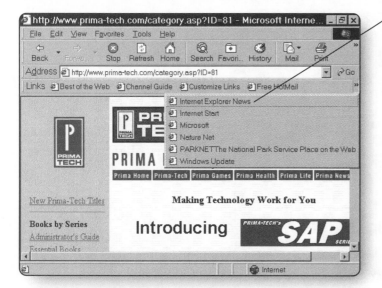

2. Click on the **Internet Start button**. The command will be executed by changing the page displayed in the browser window.

NOTE

The hidden buttons on other toolbars work much the same way. Hold the mouse pointer over a button to see which command it will execute.

Rearranging Toolbar Buttons

If you don't like the order in which buttons appear on the toolbar, you can easily change it. You can also add or remove buttons to suit your needs.

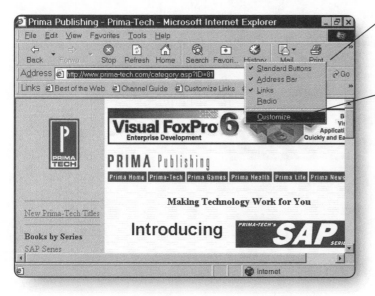

1. Right-click on an empty area of the **toolbar**. A shortcut menu will appear.

2. Click on **Customize**. The Customize Toolbar dialog box will appear.

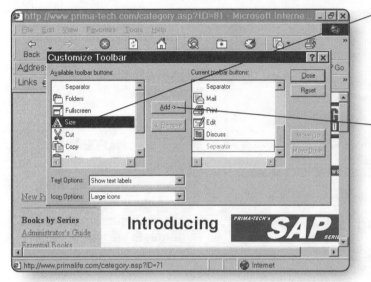

3. Click on a **button** in the Available toolbar buttons list box to select the button you want to add to the toolbar. The button will be highlighted.

4. Click on Add. The button will be added to the Current toolbar buttons list box.

NOTE

If you want to hide the text that appears below the toolbar buttons, select No text labels from the Text Options drop-down list.

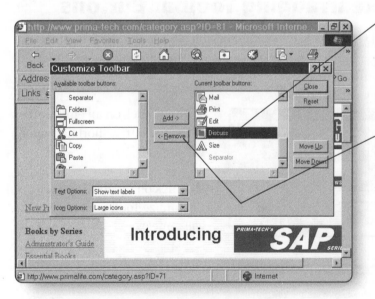

5. Click on a **button** in the Current toolbar buttons list box to remove a button from the toolbar. The button will be selected.

6. Click on Remove. The button will be removed and will appear in the Available toolbar buttons list box.

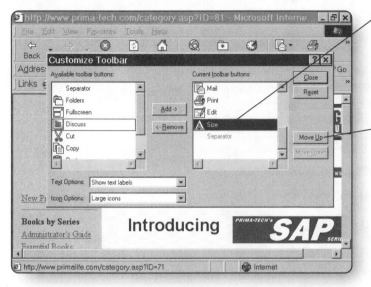

7. Click on a **button** in the Current toolbar buttons scroll box if you want to move it to a different order on the toolbar. The button will be selected.

8. Click on **Move Up** or **Move Down**. The button will move up one place or move down one place in the Current toolbar buttons list box. Moving up corresponds to moving the button to the left on the toolbar. Moving down corresponds to moving the button to the right on the toolbar.

9. Click on **Close**. Your changes will be applied and the toolbar will appear showing the changes you made.

Playing Hide and Seek with Toolbars

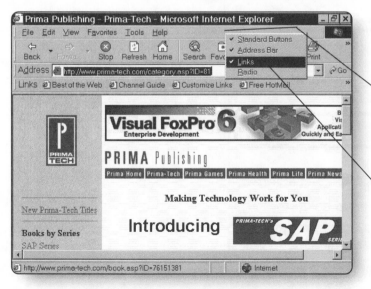

It's easy to show and hide toolbars. It's only a right-click away.

1. Right-click on an empty area of the **menu bar** or any **toolbar**. A shortcut menu will appear. Notice the following:

◆ A check mark next to a menu item means that the toolbar is displayed. To hide the toolbar, click on its menu command.

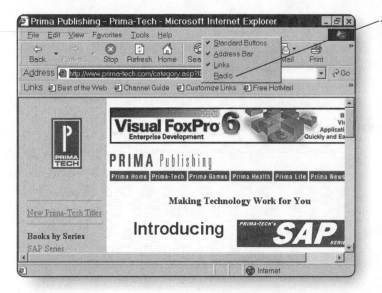

✦ An item that does not have a check mark next to it is not displayed. To display the toolbar, click on its menu command.

Moving the Position of a Toolbar

To make more room in the browser window, you can move the toolbars and the menu bar around. If you move a toolbar so that it is out of your way, you can move it again later to redisplay more of the toolbar. You have several options for moving toolbars around. Follow these steps to get comfortable moving toolbars around the top of the browser:

1. **Place** the **mouse pointer** over the vertical line to the left of a toolbar. The mouse pointer changes to a horizontal double arrow.

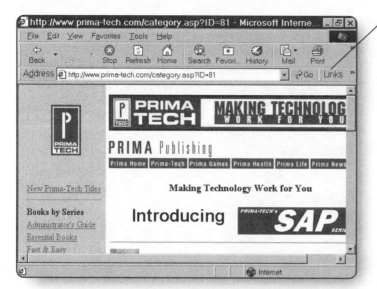

2. Click and hold the **mouse pointer** and **drag** the **toolbar** to the desired location; then release the mouse button. The toolbar will be moved.

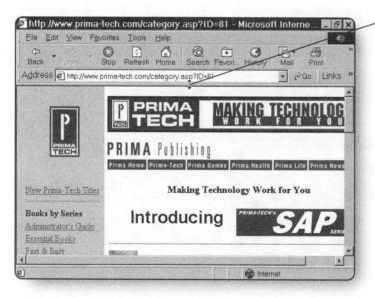

3. Place the **mouse pointer** at the bottom of the stack of toolbars. The mouse pointer will change to a vertical double arrow.

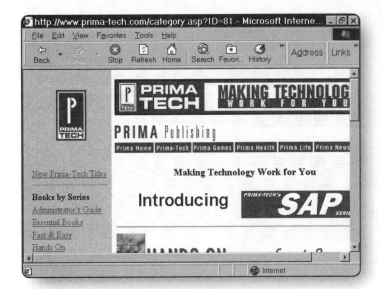

4. Click and hold the mouse pointer and drag the mouse up. The toolbar at the bottom of the stack will be placed to the right of the toolbar above it.

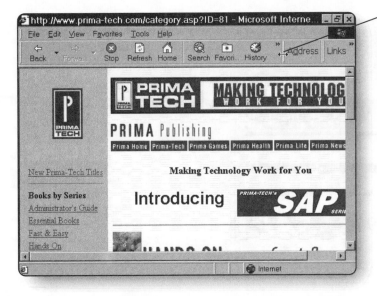

5. Place the mouse pointer over the vertical line between two toolbars. The mouse pointer will change to a horizontal double arrow.

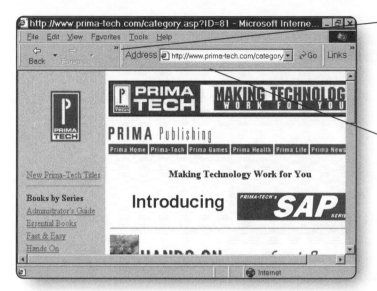

6. Click and hold the **mouse pointer** and **drag** the **mouse** to the right or the left. One toolbar will become longer and the other will become shorter.

7. Drag the **mouse pointer** down to redisplay the toolbars on separate levels.

Changing the Size of Toolbar Buttons

If you like the style of the toolbar buttons in Microsoft Office applications, you can change the Internet Explorer toolbar buttons so that they have the same look.

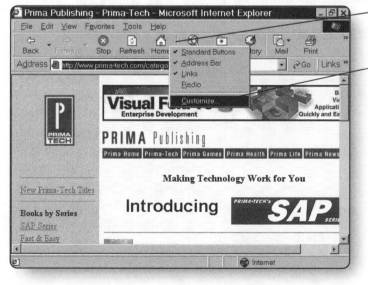

1. Right click on a **toolbar**. A menu will appear.

2. Click on **Customize**. The Customize Toolbar dialog box will open.

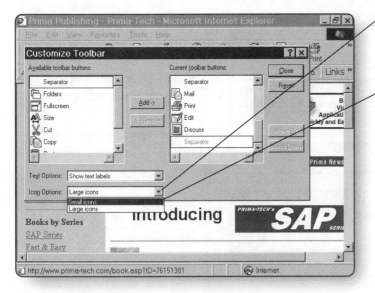

3. **Click** on the **down arrow** next to the Icon Options list box. A list of icon options will appear.

4. **Click** on **Small Icons**. The option will appear in the list box.

5. **Click** on **Close**.

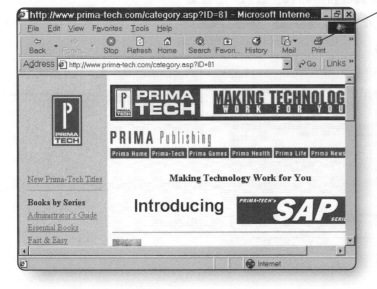

The smaller buttons will be displayed in the toolbar.

MAKING WEB PAGE TEXT MORE READABLE

After reading through a few Web pages, you may find that the size of the text on the page is not to your liking. If you have trouble reading the words on the page, you can make the text larger. If you want to fit more words into the browser window, make the text smaller.

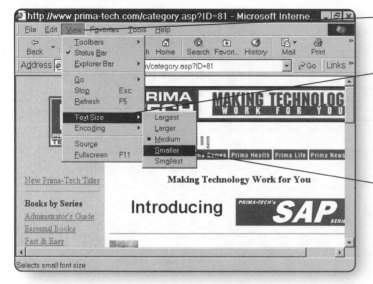

1. Click on **View**. The View menu will appear.

2. Click on **Text Size**. A drop-down menu will appear. The text size that Internet Explorer displays will be checked on the menu.

3. Click on a **font size**. The displayed text size in the browser window will change. This change will only be used while the browser is open. When you close the browser and then re-open it, the default font size will be used.

WORKING WITH BROWSER HISTORY

Knowing where you've been helps you plan your next journey by making it easier for you to go directly to sites of interest or importance. It can also help you avoid some of those sites that you don't need to see twice. Internet Explorer uses the History list to keep track of places you've been.

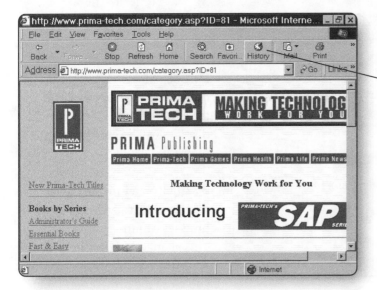

Displaying Your Internet History

1. Click on the **History button**. The History list will appear in the Explorer Bar on the left side of the browser window. The Today list will expand to show the page you are currently viewing.

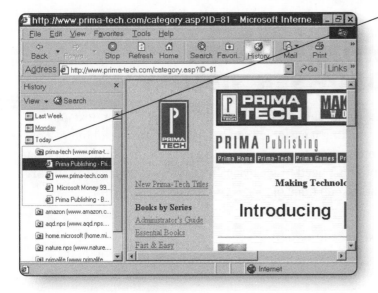

2. Click on the **time period** that you want to view. The list will expand to display the Web sites that you visited during that time period.

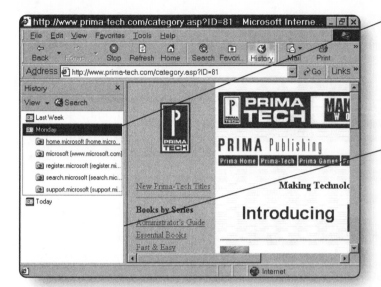

3. Click on a Web site. The list will expand to display a list of the Web pages that you visited at that Web site.

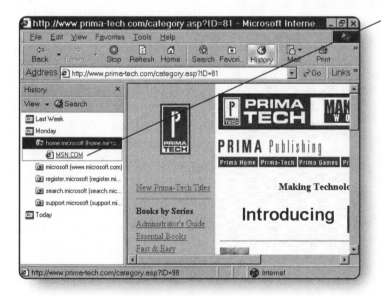

4. Click on a Web page. Internet Explorer will retrieve the Web page and display it on the right side of the browser window.

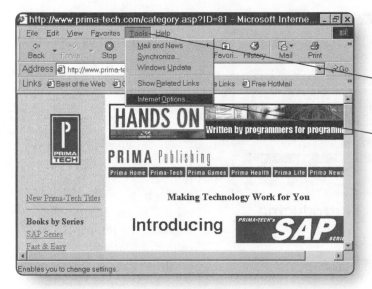

Changing Your History Settings

1. **Click** on **Tools**. The Tools menu will appear.

2. **Click** on **Internet Options**. The Internet Options dialog box will open and the General tab will be on top.

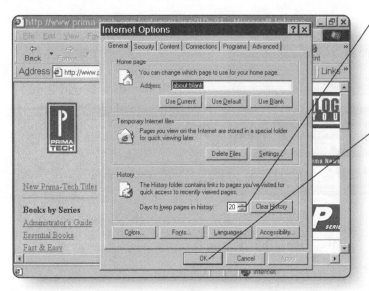

3. **Click** on the **up** or **down arrows** in the History section. The number of days that Web pages are stored in the history file will change.

4. **Click** on **OK**. The dialog box will close and you will be returned to the browser.

5 Browsing Your Computer with Internet Explorer

While surfing the Internet, you might want to take a peek at what's going on with your computer or preview a graphics file. You may think that you have to open a separate application (like Windows Explorer or Media Player), but you can save yourself a few mouse clicks and use Internet Explorer instead. With the introduction of Windows 98, the Internet Explorer browser works with your computer's operating system so that you can browse from one familiar interface. In this chapter, you'll learn how to:

+ Send an e-mail message from the browser

+ Display and navigate to drives and folders on your computer

+ Use Internet Explorer to start applications installed on your computer

+ Preview a variety of file formats

SENDING E-MAIL MESSAGES

If you don't want to switch gears or use the mouse strokes to open your e-mail application, you can send an e-mail message from the Internet Explorer browser.

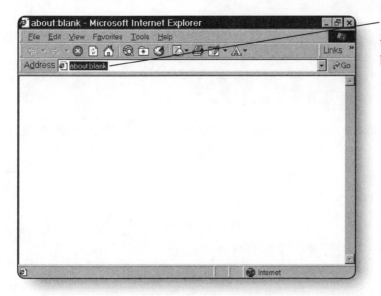

1. Click in the **Address bar**. The text that appears in the Address bar is selected.

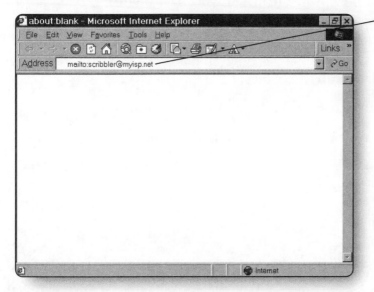

2. Type **mailto:** and the **e-mail address** of the person to whom you want to send a message.

3. Press **Enter**. (You can also click on the Go button.)

TIP

To hide the Go button, display the Advanced tab of the Options dialog box and clear the Show Go button in Address bar checkbox.

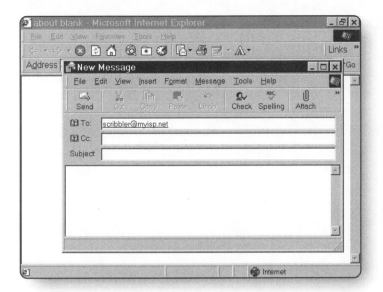

A New Message window for your default e-mail program will open and the e-mail address you typed will appear in the To field.

NOTE

To learn more about sending e-mail messages with Outlook Express, see Chapter 11, "Handling E-mail."

OPENING FOLDERS

Using Internet Explorer to browse the contents of your computer is just as easy as using Windows Explorer. It has the added advantage of allowing you to preview a number of file formats without having to open another application.

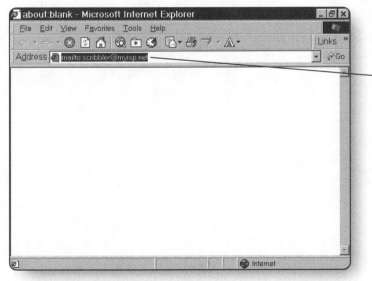

Typing the Path Name

1. Click in the **Address bar**. The text that appears in the Address bar is selected.

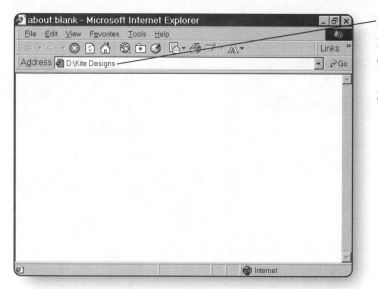

2. Type the **drive** and **path name** of the folder you want to open.

3. Press Enter.

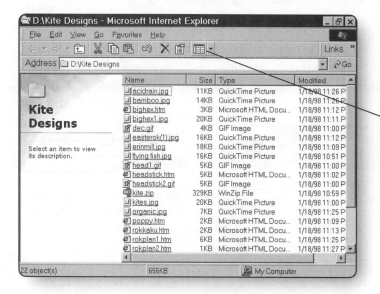

The contents of the folder will appear on the right side of the browser window.

TIP

To change the way files and folders display in the browser window, click the down arrow next to the Views button and select a different view.

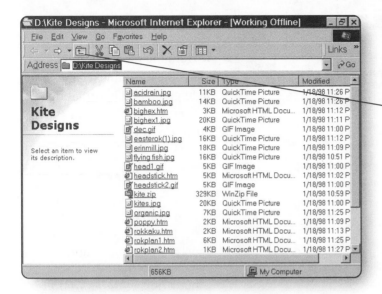

Browsing the Contents of Your Computer

1. Click on the **Up button**. The contents of the directory or drive encompassing the selected directory will appear in the browser window.

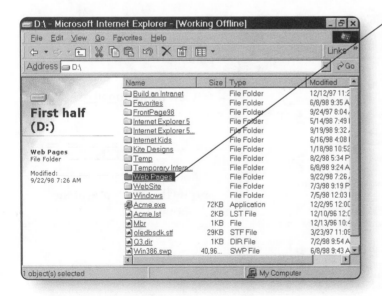

2. Click on a **folder**. The list of files contained in that folder will display.

TIP

Use the Back and Forward buttons to move between places on your computer that you've already visited. You can also use the drop-down arrow to the right of the Address bar.

Previewing Files

1. Hold the **mouse pointer** over a file. The file name will be highlighted and information about the file will appear at the left side of the browser window.

NOTE

If the preview pane is not displayed on the left side of the browser window, click on the View menu and make sure there is a check mark next to the as Web Page command.

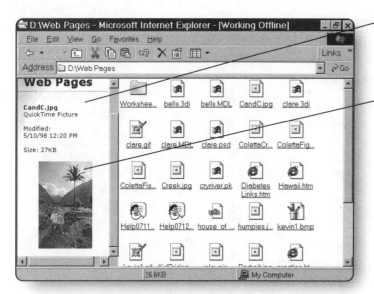

2. You can preview several types of files in the preview pane:

✦ View a thumbnail of a graphic image.

NOTE

Animated GIFs display only the first frame of the animation.

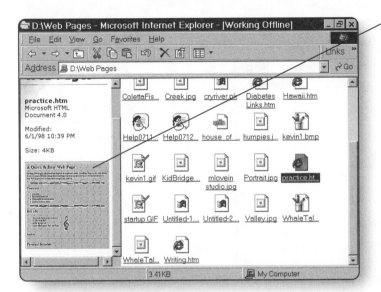

+ View a thumbnail of a Web page.

STARTING APPLICATIONS

When you don't want to go through the mouse clicks to open a program from the Start menu or from your desktop, use the Internet Explorer Address bar.

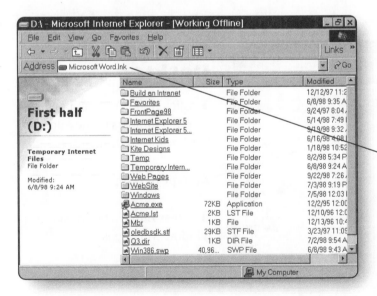

Typing Shortcut Names

1. Click in the **Address bar**. The text in the Address bar is selected.

2. Type the name of the **shortcut** followed by .lnk.

3. Press Enter.

TIP

The shortcut name is the same as the program name found on the Start menu.

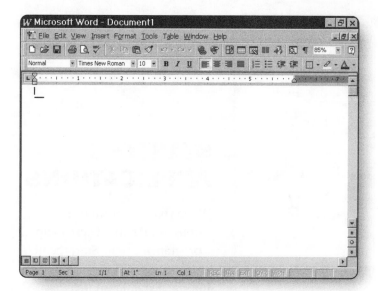

The selected application will open.

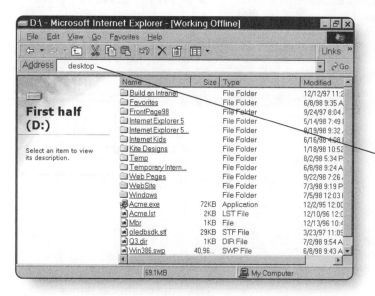

Viewing the Desktop

1. Click in the **Address bar**. The text that appears in the Address bar is selected.

2. Type **desktop**.

3. Press **Enter**. The "Desktop" window will appear.

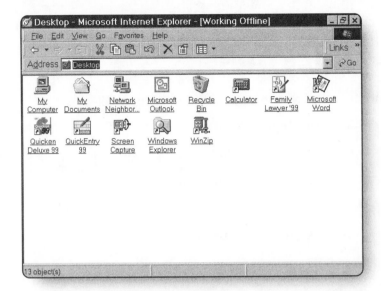

The list of icons, folders, and files that appear on your desktop will appear in the browser window.

PART II REVIEW QUESTIONS

1. What are the different ways that you can access Web pages from the Address Bar? *See "Starting from the Address Bar" in Chapter 3.*

2. How do you use hyperlinks to move from Web page to Web page? *See "Navigating between Web Pages" in Chapter 3.*

3. What is the purpose of the Back and Forward buttons? *See "Navigating between Web Pages" in Chapter 3.*

4. What types of information can you find on the Status bar? *See "Keeping Track of Things with the Status Bar" in Chapter 3.*

5. How do you change the page that first appears when you open the Internet Explorer browser? *See "Setting Your Home Page" in Chapter 4.*

6. Is it possible to change the buttons that appear on the toolbar? *See "Working with Toolbars" in Chapter 4.*

7. How can you change the font size that appears on Web pages? *See "Making Web Page Text More Readable" in Chapter 4.*

8. Is it possible to send an e-mail message without opening your e-mail program? *See "Sending E-mail Messages" in Chapter 5.*

9. How do you browse through the files and folders on your computer using the Internet Explorer browser? *See "Opening Folders" in Chapter 5.*

10. How do you open applications installed on your computer using the browser? *See "Starting Applications" in Chapter 5.*

PART III

Surfing the Web with the Internet Explorer Browser

6 Searching and Saving

As you click your way through the Internet, you'll come across many interesting Web sites. If you want to store this information, you can always keep a note of the Web site address so that you can go back to it over and over again. But what if you want to keep some of the treasures that you've found? What if the information you've found during your journeys just doesn't quite measure up to your needs? In this chapter, you'll learn how to:

✦ Store entire or portions of Web pages on your computer's hard drive

✦ Print copies of Web pages

✦ Share Web pages with friends and colleagues by e-mail

✦ Look for interesting Web sites using Search Engines

✦ Use File Transfer Protocol to retrieve files

SAVING FILES

Saving a Web page, or just a particular element on a Web page, allows you to keep a permanent copy of it on your computer's hard drive. By doing this, you can view the page or element in any application that supports these types of files. You can also make changes to these files. If you plan to use them, you must make sure you have the permission of the original creator.

Storing Web Pages on Your Hard Drive

1. **Display** the **page** you want to save.

2. **Click** on **File**. The File menu will appear.

3. **Click** on **Save As**. The Save Web Page dialog box will appear.

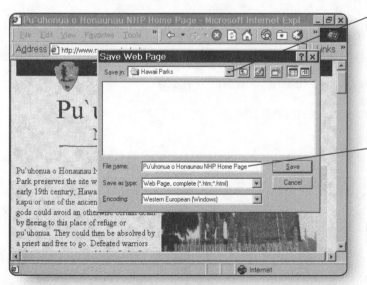

4. **Click** on the **down arrow** next to the Save in: list box and click on the directory to which you want to save the file. The directory will appear in the Save in list box.

5. **Type** a **file name** for the file in the File name text box if you don't want to use the default file name. Internet Explorer uses the title given to the Web page by its originator.

6. **Choose** one of the following **options** from the Save as type list box:

✦ **Web Page, complete** saves all of the elements (text, graphics, sounds, and other multimedia elements) needed to display the entire page.

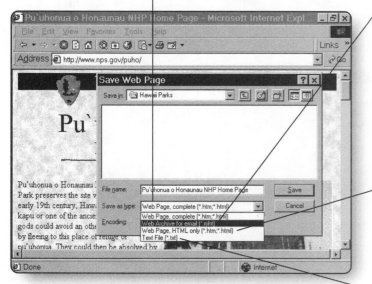

✦ **Web Archive** for e-mail makes a single picture of the Web page so that it can be viewed from within the message pane of an e-mail program. This only works with e-mail programs that can create and display HTML-formatted messages, such as Outlook Express.

✦ **Web Page, HTML only** saves the text and HTML information on the page, but not pictures, sounds, or other linked files.

✦ **Text File** saves only the text on the page so that it can be displayed in a text editor (such as Notepad).

7. **Click** on the **Save button**. The file will be stored in the designated directory on your computer.

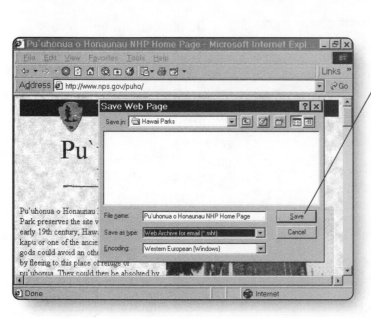

Saving Web Page Elements

1. **Right-click** on the Web page **element** that you want to save. A shortcut menu will appear.

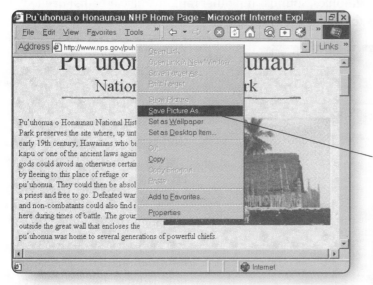

2. **Choose** from one of the following save **commands**. A Save dialog box will appear.

✦ **Save Background As** will save the image used as the Web page background.

✦ **Save Picture As** will save the image on the Web page.

NOTE

Before you save images you find on the Web, make sure you have the permission of the person who created the Web page.

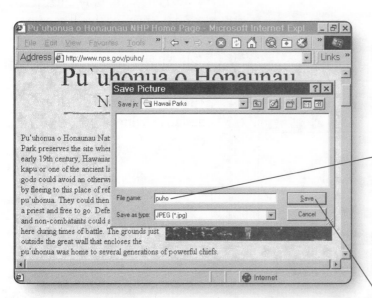

3. **Click** on the **down arrow** next to the Save in: list box and **click** on the **directory** to which you want to save the file. The directory will appear in the Save in list box.

4. **Type** a **file name** for the element in the File name text box. If this field is already filled in, you can accept the file name unchanged or you can give the file a different name.

5. **Click** on **Save**. The element will be saved to your computer in the directory specified.

PRINTING PAGES

Even though we live in an electronic world, it is sometimes more convenient to have a paper copy of a document.

Sending a Page to Your Printer

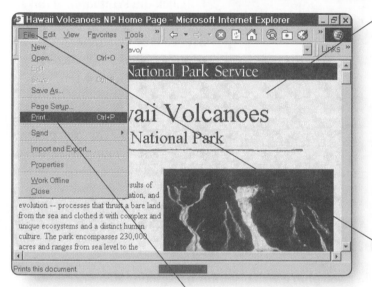

1. **Display** the **Web page** that you want to print. The page will appear in the browser window.

NOTE

If the Web page contains frames and you do not want to print all of the frames, click in the frame that you want to print.

2. **Click** on **File**. The File menu will appear.

3. **Click** on **Print**. The Print dialog box will appear.

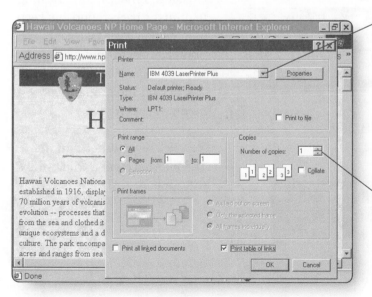

4. **Click** on the **down arrow** to the left of the Name list box. A list of printers installed on your computer will appear.

5. **Click** on the **printer** to which you want to print the Web page. The printer will be selected.

6. **Click** the **up** and **down arrows** to select the number of copies of the Web page that you want to print.

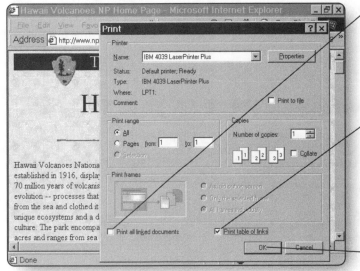

7. Click the **Print all linked documents checkbox** if you also want to print all the Web pages that are linked to the Web page displayed in the browser window.

8. Click the **Print table of links checkbox** if you want to print a list of all the hyperlinks contained in the Web page displayed in the browser window.

9. Click on **OK**. The Web page will be sent to your printer and a paper copy will appear.

Printing Backgrounds with the Web Page

When you print a Web page, any background colors or background images will not appear on the printed page. You can change Internet Explorer's setting to print the background, but keep in mind that it will take your printer longer to output the page.

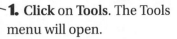

1. Click on **Tools**. The Tools menu will open.

2. Click on **Internet Options**. The Internet Options dialog box will appear.

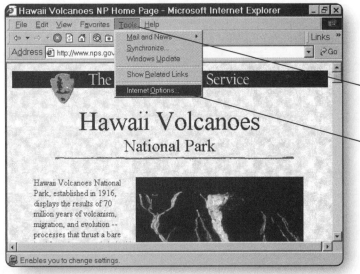

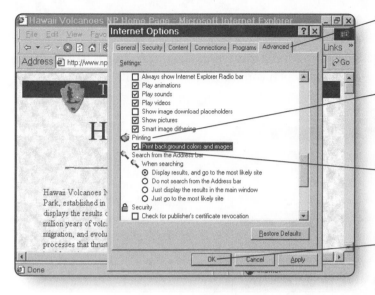

3. Click on the **Advanced tab**. The Advanced options will appear.

4. **Scroll** to the bottom of the **list**. The Printing options will appear.

5. **Click** on **Print background colors and images**. A check will appear in the box.

6. **Click** on **OK**. The settings will be applied and the page can be printed so that background colors and images also print.

Changing the Page Layout Settings

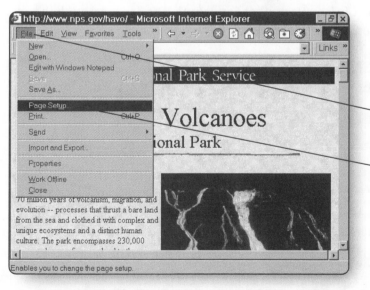

If you don't like the way the Web page appears on the printed page, you can easily change some of its layout settings.

1. **Click** on **File**. The File menu will open.

2. **Click** on **Page Setup**. The Page Setup dialog box will appear.

3. Select the correct **paper size** from the Size drop-down list.

4. Select the **source tray** where the printer needs to look for the paper on which you want the file to print.

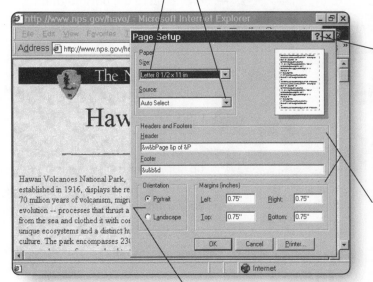

Click on the question mark (?) and then click on the Headers and Footers section. A screen tip with the header and footer codes and a description will appear.

5. Add header and footer information to the printed page.

6. Click on Portrait or Landscape. The paper orientation will be adjusted accordingly.

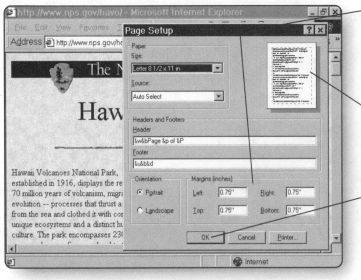

7. Click in the **Margins fields** and type a new value for the margins.

The thumbnail view shows how the page will look with the setting you choose.

8. Click on OK. Your new settings will be applied and you can print the page again.

E-MAILING WEB PAGES TO YOUR FRIENDS

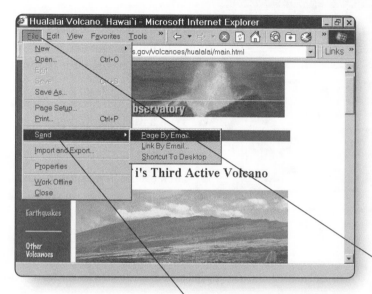

When you find a Web page that would interest a friend or colleague, you can easily send them just the URL address for the page. Better yet, you can send them the whole Web page: graphics, links, everything.

1. Display the **Web page** that you want to send to someone else. The page will appear in the browser window.

2. Click on **File**. The File menu will appear.

3. Click on **Send**. A drop-down menu will appear.

4. Choose one of the following menu **commands**:

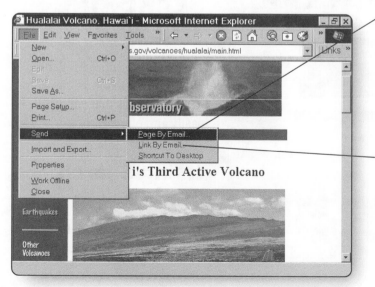

✦ **Page By Email** will send the entire Web page. Use this command if the person to whom you are sending the e-mail has an e-mail application that supports HTML (such as Outlook Express).

✦ **Link By Email** will send just the URL address of the Web page. Use this command if the person to whom you are sending the e-mail has an e-mail application that does not support HTML (such as an older version of Eudora).

A message dialog box for your default e-mail program will appear.

5. Type the **e-mail address** of the person to whom you want to send the Web page in the To text box.

6. Type a **message** in the message area, if desired.

7. Click on the Send button. The message will be stored in your e-mail program until you tell the program to send the message.

NOTE

To learn more about sending e-mail messages, see Chapter 11, "Handling E-mail."

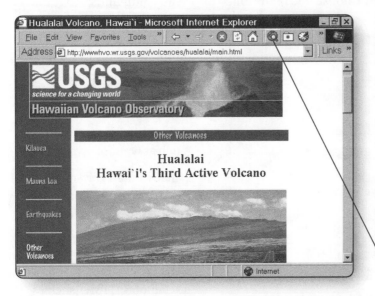

SEARCHING THE WEB

The search facilities available with Internet Explorer can help you find things that you want easily and effortlessly.

Using Search Engines

1. Click on the **Search button** to activate the Search bar.

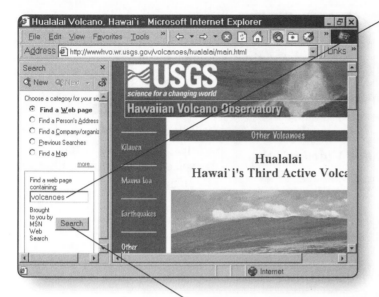

2. Click in the **search text box** and **type** a few **words** to describe the type of information that you need.

TIP

When you surround your search words with quotation marks, the search engine will return only those results that contain all of the words in your search.

3. Click on the **Search button**. The search engine will compile a list of Web pages that match your search terms.

NOTE

Not every search engine labels these buttons the same way. Some may call it the Find button, while others may call it the Submit or Seek button.

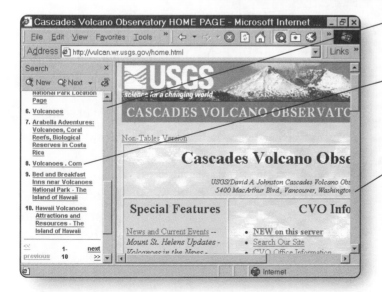

4. Scroll through the list of **search results**.

5. Click on a search result **hyperlink**. The linked Web page will download into the right side of the browser window.

6. Look through the **Web page** to see whether it contains the information for which you are looking.

7. Click on **next**. The Search bar will display the next group of search results.

Performing Quick Searches from the Address Bar

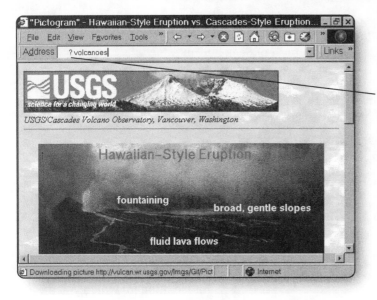

1. Click in the **Address bar**. The text in the Address bar will be highlighted.

2. Type a **question mark (?)** followed by a space and the text that describes what you want to find.

3. Press Enter. A list of search results will appear.

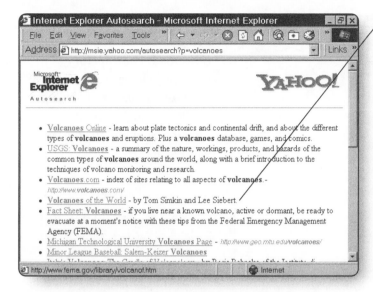

4. Scroll through the **list** of search results and **click** on a **hyperlink** that matches the information for which you are searching.

TIP

Use the Back button to return to the search page.

USING FTP TO RETRIEVE FILES

Internet Explorer 5 comes with a built-in File Transfer Protocol (FTP) utility that makes it easy to download files from FTP sites. You no longer need a separate application to gain access to these sites.

1. Click in the **Address bar** and **type** the **FTP address** of the site that contains the files you want to download.

2. Press Enter. You will be connected to the FTP site in the browser window.

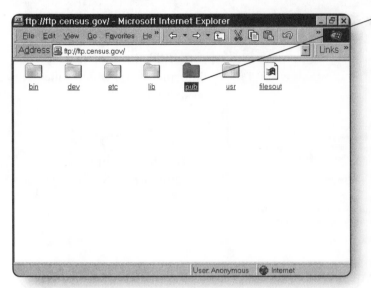

3. Click on the **directory** that contains the file you want to download. The directory contents will be listed in the browser window. You may need to click through several directories to find the file you want.

TIP

There is usually a directory list or readme document in each FTP site that will tell you what is contained within each directory.

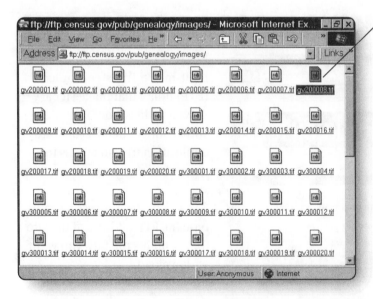

4. Click on the **file** you want to download. The File Download dialog box will open.

TIP

You can use the Back, Forward, and Up buttons to navigate through an FTP site.

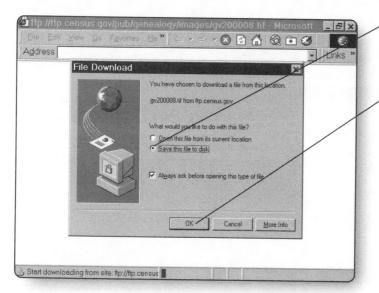

5. Click on the Save this program to disk button. The option will be selected.

6. Click on OK. The Save As dialog box will appear.

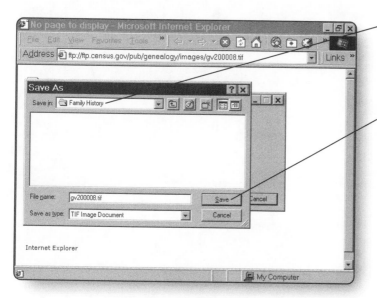

7. Select the directory where you want to save the file. The directory will appear in the Save in list box.

8. Click on Save. The File Download dialog box will appear.

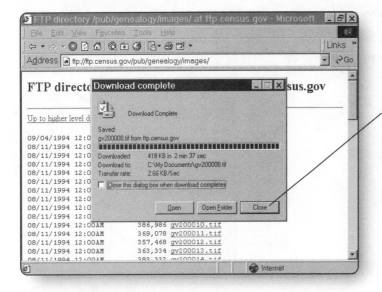

9. Wait while the file downloads to your computer. The Download complete dialog box will signal the end of the transfer.

10. Click on **Close**. The file can be found on your computer in the directory that you specified.

7 Working with Favorites

If you visit a number of Web sites on a regular basis, you'll want to keep a list of those sites for future reference. By using a tool called Favorites, you can keep all of the Web pages organized in one convenient place. The Favorites feature can categorize sites by topic, keep track of the URL addresses for preferred sites, and make it easier to return to them in future sessions. You can also share your Favorites with friends and view Web pages when you are not connected to the Internet. In this chapter, you'll learn how to:

✦ Create and view a Favorite

✦ Organize your list of Favorites

✦ Customize the Links bar

✦ Share a list of Favorites between computers

✦ View Web pages while working offline

GETTING STARTED WITH FAVORITES

As you travel the Internet, you'll come across a wealth of interesting and informative Web sites. When you find a Web site that you think you'll want to visit again, you'll need to make a note of its URL address. You could always write the URL address on a piece of paper, but rather than create a trail of misplaced notes, add the Web site to your list of Favorites.

Adding a Site to Your List of Favorites

1. **Access** the **page** you want to add to your collection of favorite pages. The Web page will appear in the browser window.

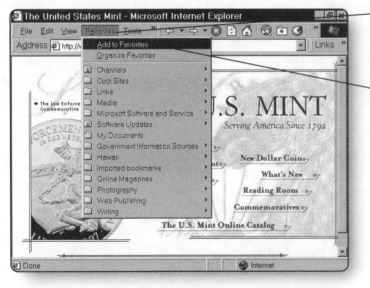

2. **Click** on **Favorites** on the menu bar. The Favorites menu will appear.

3. **Click** on **Add to Favorites**. The Add Favorite dialog box will open.

4. Leave the **default name** for the Web page in the Name text box or **type** in a **different name**. Changing the name does not affect the URL address.

TIP

To delete text, select it and press the Delete key. To insert text, click the mouse in the place where you want to add the text; then begin typing.

5. Click on OK. The page will be added to your list of Favorites.

NOTE

Internet Explorer puts the newest Favorite at the bottom of the list. You'll learn how to manage your list of Favorites later in this chapter.

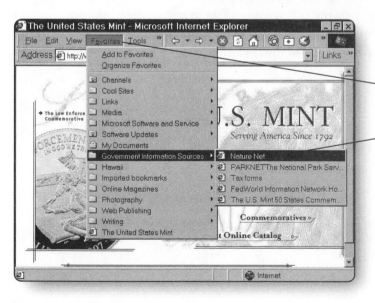

Viewing a Favorite Page

1. Click on **Favorites**. The Favorites menu will appear.

2. Click on the **Favorite** that you want to view.

NOTE

To view the Favorites that are organized into folders, move the mouse pointer to highlight the appropriate folder. Select the desired Web site from the drop-down menu.

The Web page will appear in the browser window.

ORGANIZING YOUR LIST OF FAVORITES

If you anticipate a long Favorites list, make it easier to find your Favorites by grouping them into folders. Internet Explorer also gives you the flexibility to change the order of Favorites within the list and to move them to different folders.

Sorting Favorites into Folders

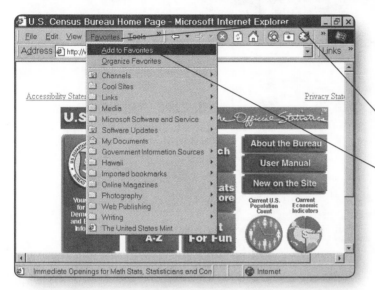

1. Access the **page** you want to add to your Favorites collection. The Web page will appear in the browser window.

2. Click on **Favorites**. The Favorites menu will appear.

3. Click on **Add to Favorites**. The Add Favorite dialog box will open.

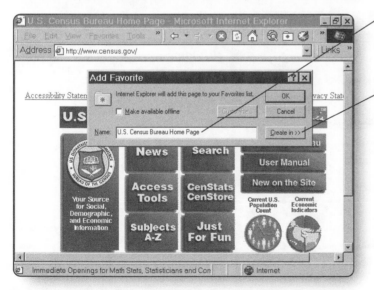

4. Leave the **default name** for the Web page in the Name text box or **type** a **different name**.

5. Click on the **Create in button**. The dialog box will expand and a list of folders found in the Favorites menu will appear.

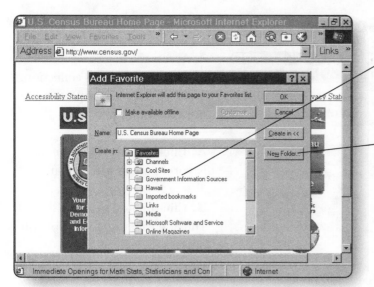

NOTE

To place a Favorite into an existing folder, click on the folder and press OK.

6. **Click** on **New Folder**. The Create New Folder dialog box will open.

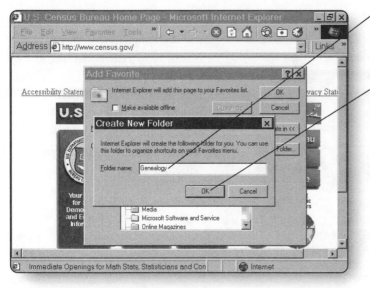

7. **Click** in the **Folder name text box** and **type** a **name** for the folder.

8. **Click** on **OK**.

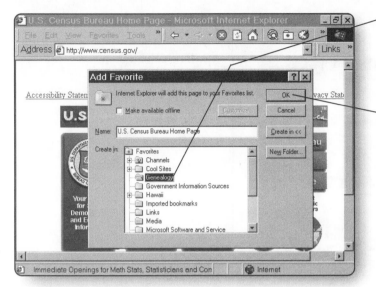

The new folder will be included in the Favorites menu and selected as the destination for the current Favorite.

9. **Click** on **OK**. The Web page will be added to the new folder in the list of Favorites.

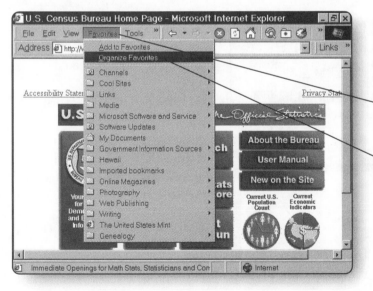

Changing the Order of Favorites

1. Click on **Favorites** to see the Favorites menu.

2. Click on **Organize Favorites**. The Organize Favorites dialog box will open.

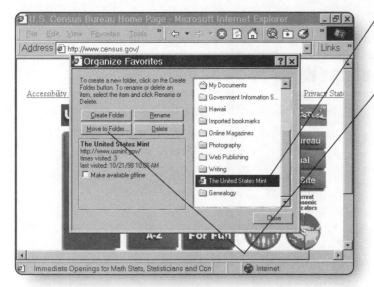

3. Click on the **Favorite** that you want to move. The Favorite will be selected.

4. Click on **Move to Folder**. The Browse for Folder dialog box will open.

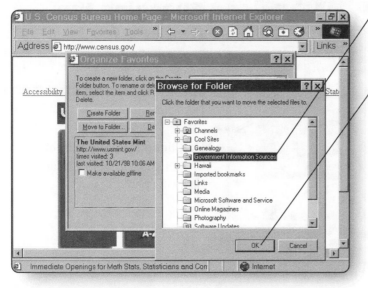

5. Click on the **folder** to which you want to move the Favorite. The folder will be selected.

6. Click on **OK**. The Favorite will be moved into the designated folder. You can also change the order in which Favorites and folders appear in the list.

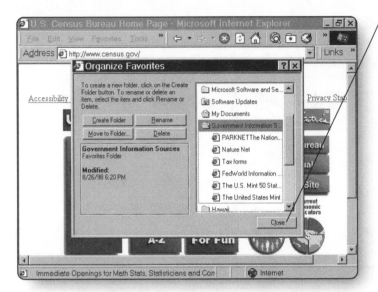

7. Click on Close. The list of Favorites will appear in the Favorites menu in the order that you specified.

ADDING FAVORITES TO THE LINKS BAR

For one-click access, add your most frequently visited Web sites to the Links bar. To make best use of the Links bar, you'll want to display it on a separate level in the browser window.

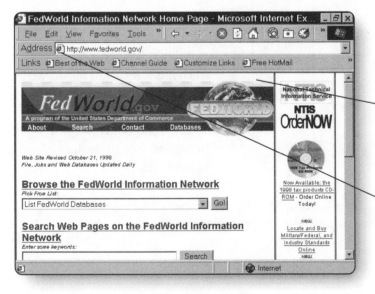

Adding a Web Page to the Links Bar

1. Open the page you want to add to the Links bar. The Web page will appear in the browser window.

2. Click and hold on the Web page icon in the Address bar. The mouse pointer will change to show that a shortcut will be made.

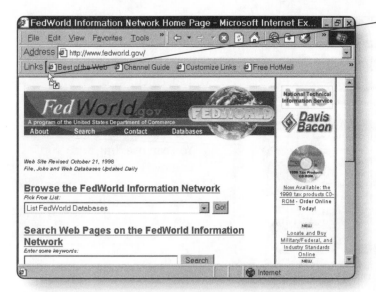

3. **Drag** the **mouse** to the location on the Links bar where you want the Web page to appear and **release** the **mouse button**. The Web page will appear as a button on the Links bar.

TIP

You can make changes to links on the Links bar. Right click on a link and view the available commands. Left click on a link to see it in the browser window.

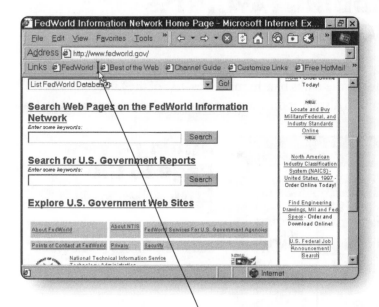

Adding a Hyperlink to the Links Bar

If you don't want to go through the trouble of clicking on a hyperlink on one page to access a page that you want to add to your Links bar, you can select the hyperlink to add the desired page to the Links bar.

1. **Click and hold** on a **hyperlink**. The hyperlink will be selected.

2. **Drag** the **mouse** to the location on the Links bar where you want to place the link and **release** the **mouse button**.

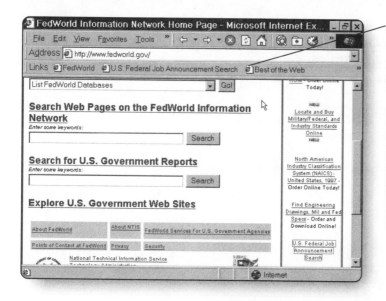

A button for the hyperlink will appear on the Links bar. Click on the button to display the Web page in the browser window.

SHARING FAVORITES WITH YOUR FRIENDS

You and your friends can easily share both Internet Explorer Favorites and Netscape Navigator Bookmarks. You can use the Internet Explorer Export feature to create an HTML file that you can send as an e-mail attachment or distribute on a floppy disk. This file can be imported into a different list of Favorites or Bookmarks, or it can be opened in a Web browser and explored like a regular Web page.

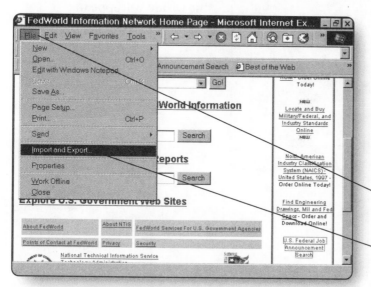

Exporting Your Favorites List

1. Click on **File**. The File menu will appear.

2. Click on **Import and Export**. The Import/Export Wizard will open.

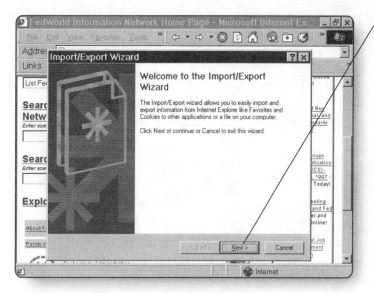

3. **Click** on **Next**. The Import/Export selection page of the wizard will appear.

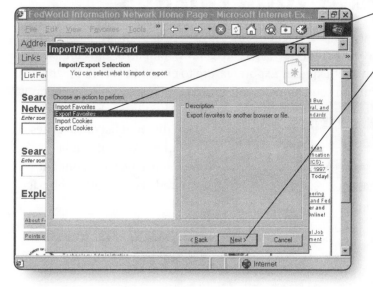

4. **Click** on **Export Favorites**. The option will be selected.

5. **Click** on **Next**. The Export Favorites Source Folder page of the wizard will appear.

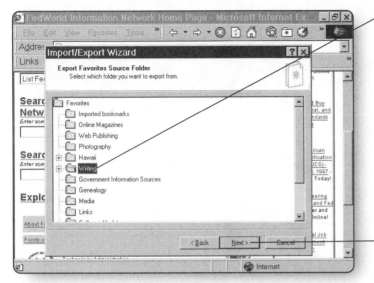

6. Click on the **folder** that contains the Favorites you wish to convert into an HTML file to share with others.

7. Click on **Next**. The Export Favorites page of the wizard will open.

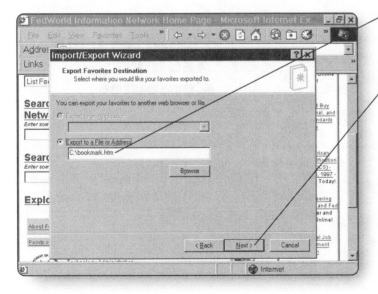

8. Change the **name** of the file, drive, and directory where you want the file stored, if needed.

9. Click on **Next**. The Completing the Import/Export Wizard page of the wizard will appear.

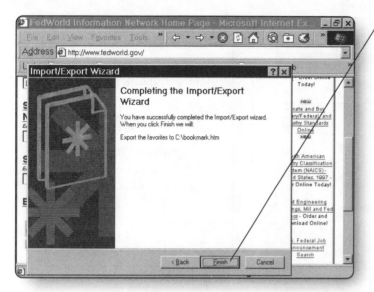

10. Click on **Finish**. The list of Favorites will be saved in the designated folder on your computer. You can now attach this file to an e-mail message and send it to a friend, or you can export it to another computer to share Favorites between computers.

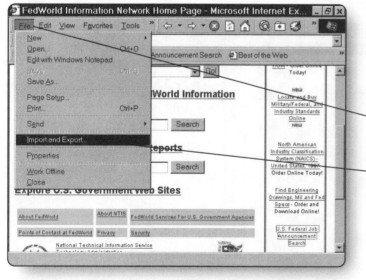

Importing Favorites from Another Computer

1. Click on **File**. The File menu will appear.

2. Click on **Import and Export**. The Import/Export Wizard will open.

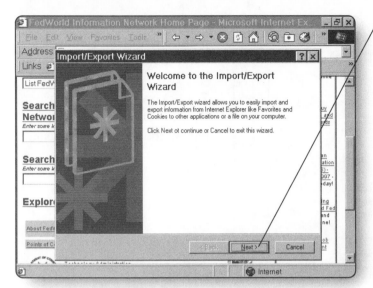

3. **Click** on **Next**. The Import/Export Selection page of the wizard will appear.

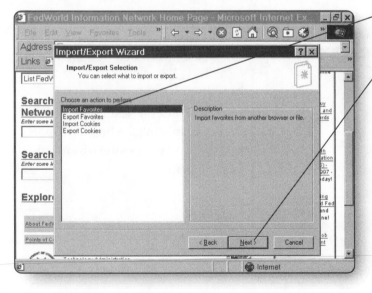

4. **Click** on **Import Favorites**. The option will be selected.

5. **Click** on **Next**. The Import Favorites Source page of the wizard will appear.

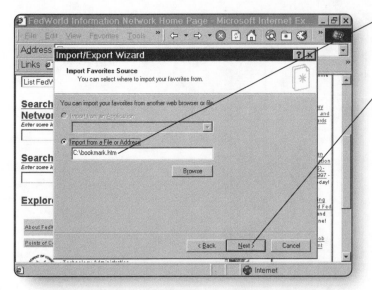

6. Type the **drive**, directory **path**, and **file name** for the file that you want to import.

7. **Click** on **Next**. The Import Favorites Destination Folder page of the wizard will appear.

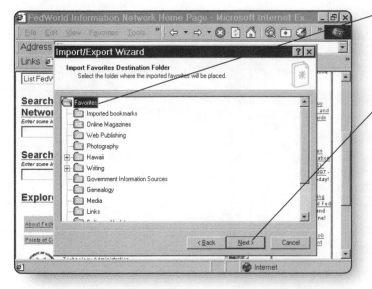

8. **Click** on the **folder** where you want the new list of Favorites stored. The folder will be selected.

9. **Click** on **Next**. The Completing the Import/Export Wizard page of the wizard will appear.

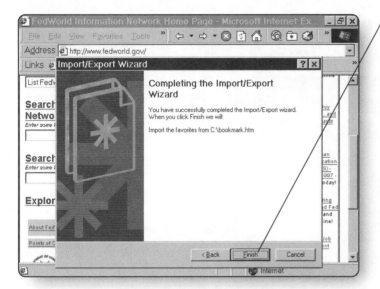

10. Click on **Finish**. The list of favorites will be imported to the list of favorites you are currently using with Internet Explorer.

VIEWING YOUR FAVORITES OFFLINE

You may wish to download the contents of your favorite Web pages to enjoy them when you have more time or to access information when an Internet connection is unavailable. Use your Favorites list to take advantage of Internet Explorer's offline browsing capabilities.

TIP

If you have an existing Favorite that you want to set up for offline viewing, right click on it in the Favorites menu. Select the Make available offline command. This starts the Offline Favorite Wizard.

Selecting Favorites
for Offline Viewing

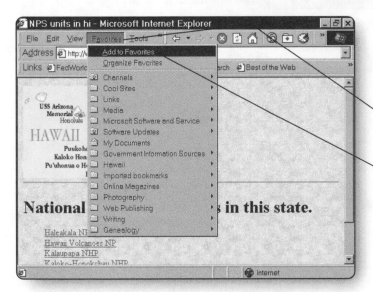

1. **Access** the **page** you want to set up for offline viewing. The Web page will appear in the browser window.

2. **Click** on **Favorites**. The Favorites menu will appear.

3. **Click** on **Add to Favorites**. The Add Favorite dialog box will open.

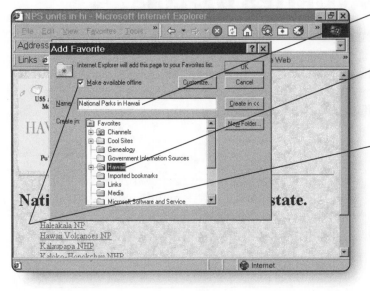

4. **Edit** the **name** of the Web page, if desired.

5. **Click** on the **folder** in which you want to place the Favorite. The folder will be selected.

6. **Click** in the **Make available offline checkbox**. A check will appear in the box.

7. **Click** on the **Customize button**. The Offline Favorite Wizard will start.

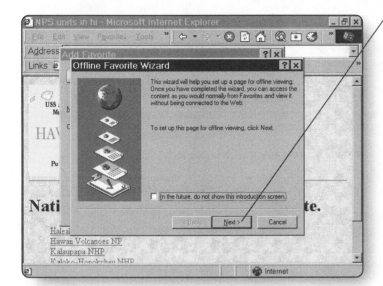

8. **Click** on **Next**. The next screen of the wizard will appear.

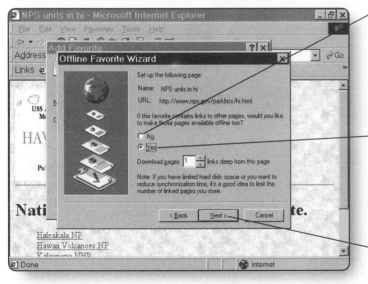

9a. **Click** on the **Yes button** if your Favorite has other links that you want to make available for offline viewing. The option will be selected.

OR

9b. **Click** on the **No button** if you wish to download only the page displayed in the browser window. The option will be selected.

10. **Click** on **Next**. The next screen of the wizard will appear.

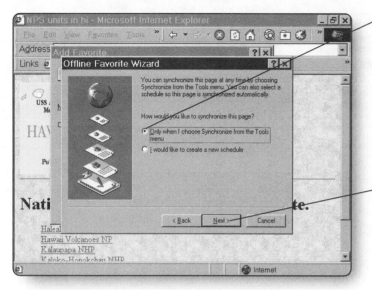

11. Click on the **Only when I choose Synchronize from the Tools menu button**. By choosing this method, you decide when to connect to the Internet to download the content from these pages. The option will be selected.

12. Click on **Next**. The final screen of the wizard will appear.

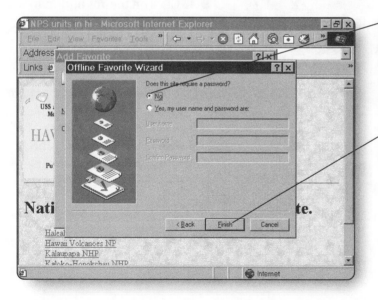

13. Click on either **Yes** or **No** to specify whether a user name and password are needed to access the Web site. The option will be selected.

14. Click on **Finish**. The Add Favorite dialog box will return.

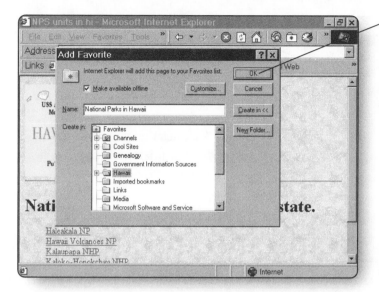

15. Click on **OK**. The Web page is now added to the Favorites list and is set up for offline viewing.

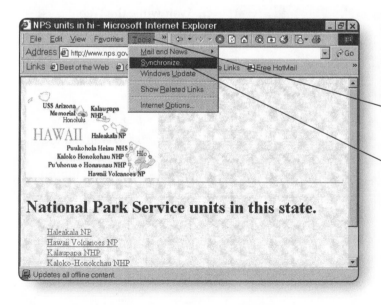

Downloading Pages for Offline Viewing

1. Click on **Tools**. The Tools menu will appear.

2. Click on **Synchronize**. The Items to Synchronize dialog box will open.

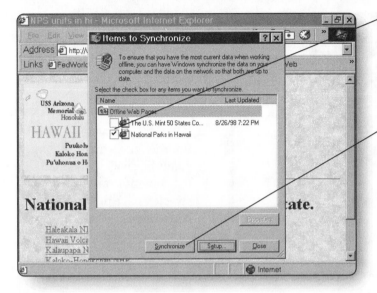

3. **Click** on the **check box** next to items for which you want to download the latest version for offline viewing. A check will appear in the box.

4. **Click** on **Synchronize**. The Synchronizing status box will open.

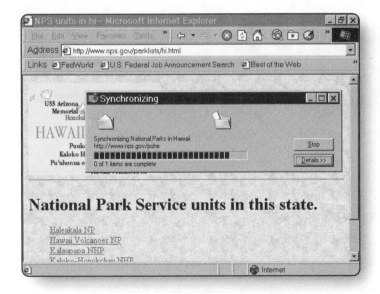

5. **Wait** while the Web pages download to your computer. When the download is complete, the status box will close.

TIP

If you want to watch the status of the download, click on the Details button.

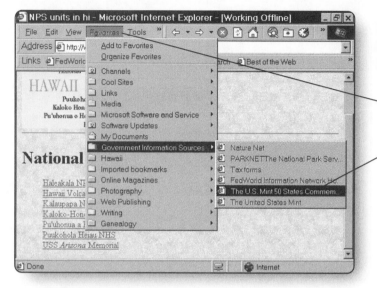

Viewing Web Pages While Offline

1. Click on **Favorites**. The Favorites menu will appear.

2. Click on the **Favorite** that you want to view offline. Those Favorites that are not available offline are grayed out.

The Web page will appear in the browser window.

NOTE

The Work Offline symbol will appear in the status bar when you are viewing a Web page and are not connected to the Internet.

8 Keeping Your Computer Safe

In an ideal world, the Internet would be free of viruses, hazards, and unwanted content. But, just like the real world we live in, the Internet world has its share of malicious prowlers. It also has some protective devices you can use to keep your computer's hardware, software, and data files safe. Internet Explorer offers built-in tools that provide security for your computer when you travel on the Internet. In this chapter, you'll learn how to:

✦ Block harmful content from downloading to your computer

✦ Use the Content Advisor to deny access to undesirable Web sites

✦ Control the use of cookies on your computer

✦ Disable downloading of multimedia elements to reduce downloading time

BLOCKING CONTENT FROM HARMFUL WEB SITES

Security zones are filters that prevent Web sites from downloading potentially dangerous material to your computer. Harmful content may include ActiveX controls, Java applets, file and font downloads, and cookies. These items present a potential hazard to your computer because they are actually small programs that are downloaded, executed, and run on your computer. The following steps show you how to set security zones so that you're protected from worrisome Web sites.

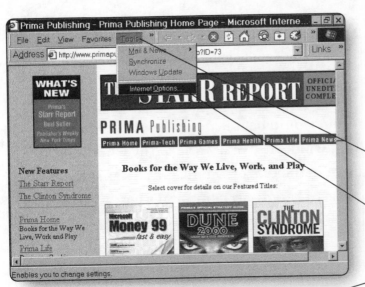

1. Click on **Tools**. The Tools menu will appear.

2. Click on **Internet Options**. The Internet Options dialog box will open.

3. Click on the **Security tab**. The Security tab will come to the top of the stack.

4. Click on **Restricted sites zone** to activate it. Notice that the security level for this zone is High and a description of the type of content that will be prevented from downloading to your computer will appear at the bottom of the dialog box.

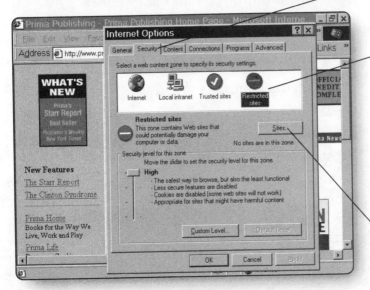

5. Click on the **Sites button**. The Restricted Sites dialog box will appear.

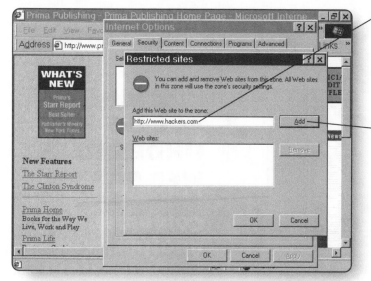

6. In the Add this Web site to the zone text box, **type** the **URL address** for the Web site that you believe might contain damaging content.

7. **Click** on **Add**. Added Web sites will not be allowed to download potentially harmful material to your computer. Content such as text, GIF files, and JPEG images will still appear in the browser.

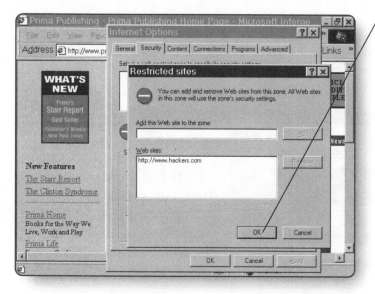

8. **Click** on **OK**. The Internet Options dialog box will appear.

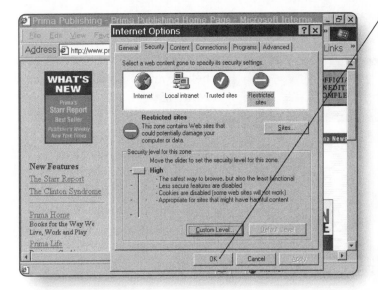

9. **Click** on **OK**. The new settings will be applied.

PREVENTING ACCESS TO UNDESIRABLE WEB SITES

The Content Advisor is a handy way to keep others from using your computer to access Web sites with content that you deem undesirable. If your children use your computer, you may want to use the Content Advisor to restrict their access to sites that contain adult material. Or you may also not want to subject yourself to sites that use profane language. Whatever your reasons, the Content Advisor will let you make your own decisions and determine a comfort level for your Web travels.

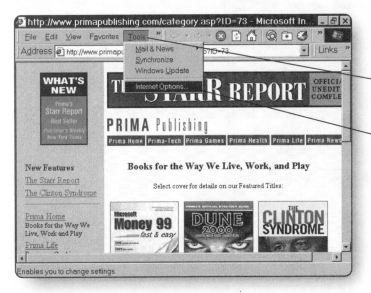

Activating the Content Advisor

1. **Click** on **Tools**. The Tools menu will appear.

2. **Click** on **Internet Options**. The Internet Options dialog box will open.

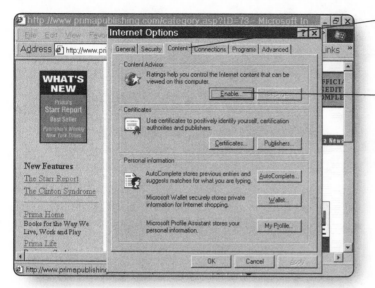

3. Click on the **Content tab**. The Content tab will come to the top of the stack.

4. Click on the **Enable button**. The Content Advisor dialog box will appear.

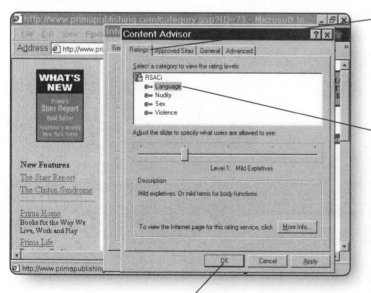

5. Click on a **ratings category**. Details about the selected ratings category will be displayed in the lower part of the dialog box.

6. Press and hold the **mouse button** on the slider bar and drag it left or right until you find the desired tolerance level for the category.

7. Release the **mouse button**. The tolerance level will be selected.

8. Click on **OK**. The Create Supervisor Password dialog box will appear.

9. Type a password.

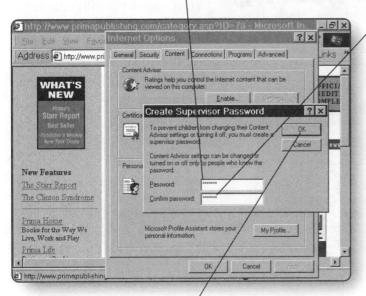

10. Type the same **password** again in the Confirm password box. This will confirm that you typed the supervisor password correctly.

NOTE

If you forget your supervisor password, you will not be able to turn the Content Advisor on and off, nor will you be able to change the ratings levels.

11. Click on **OK**. This creates your supervisor password and provides you with sole access to the Content Advisor. A confirmation dialog box will appear.

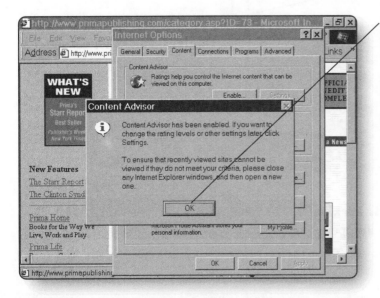

12. Click on **OK** to confirm the new Content Advisor Settings. The Internet Options dialog box will reappear on your screen and the Enable button will change to a Disable button.

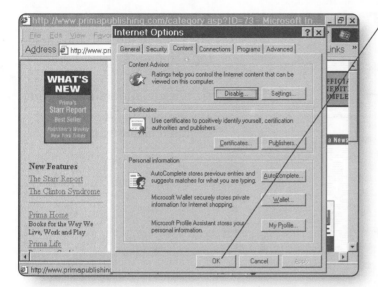

13. Click on **OK**. The new Content Advisor Setting will be applied and sites that contain content that are outside your settings will not appear in the browser if someone tries to access the site.

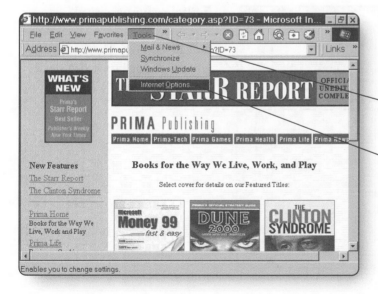

Changing the Supervisor Password

1. Click on **Tools**. The Tools menu will appear.

2. Click on **Internet Options**. The Internet Options dialog box will appear.

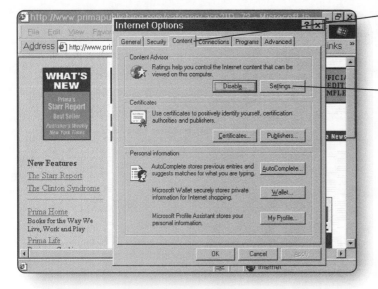

3. Click on the **Content tab**. The Content tab will come to the top of the stack.

4. Click on the **Settings button**. The Supervisor Password Required dialog box will appear.

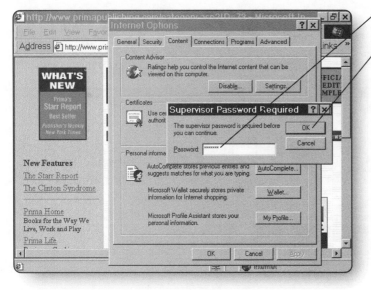

5. Type your **password**.

6. Click on **OK**. The Content Advisor dialog box will appear.

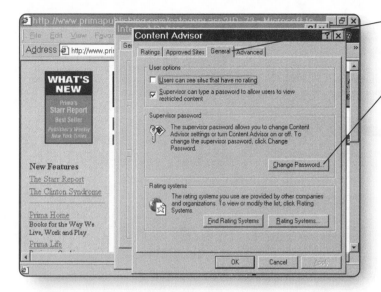

7. **Click** on the **General tab**. The General tab will come to the top of the stack.

8. **Click** on the **Change Password button**. The Change Supervisor Password dialog box will appear.

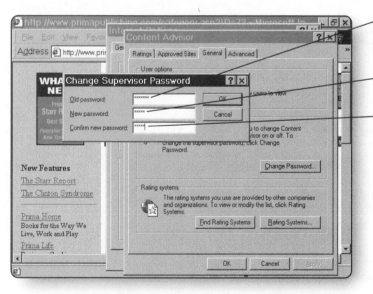

9. **Type** your **current (Old) password**.

10. **Type** a **New password**.

11. **Type** the **new password** a second time to confirm it.

12. **Click** on **OK**. A Content Advisor message box will notify you that the password has been changed.

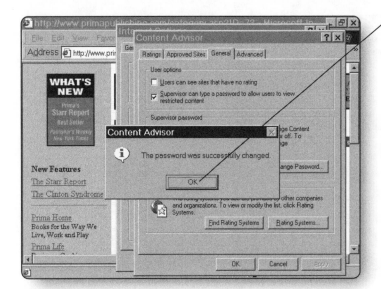

13. **Click** on **OK**. The Content Advisor dialog box will return.

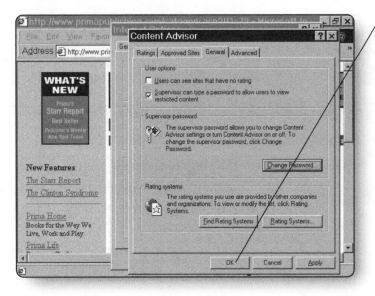

14. **Click** on **OK**. The Internet Options dialog box will appear.

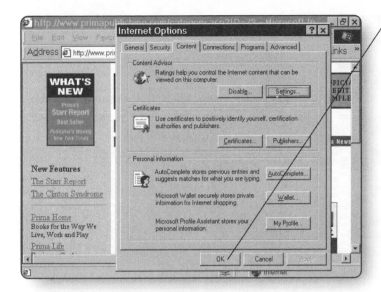

15. Click on **OK**. Your new supervisor password will be enabled.

NOTE

You can turn off the Content Advisor by clicking on the Disable button. Be aware that this will allow unrestricted access to all Web sites. You will need to type your supervisor password in the dialog box that appears.

SECURING THE COOKIE JAR

Cookies are small files stored on your computer that contain information about your visits to a Web site. They may allow you to continue browsing the site from the place where you concluded your previous visit, or they may remember information that you supplied to the site on a previous visit. You can decide individually or universally as to whether to accept cookies that ask to be downloaded to your computer.

1. Click on **Tools**. The Tools menu will appear.

2. Click on **Internet Options**. The Internet Options dialog box will open.

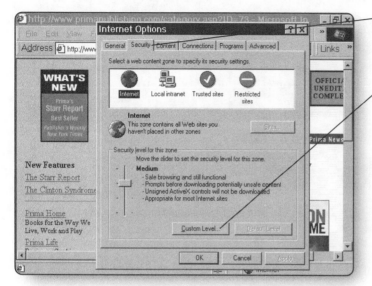

3. Click on the **Security tab**. The Security tab will come to the top of the stack.

4. Click on **Custom Level**. The Security Settings dialog box will appear.

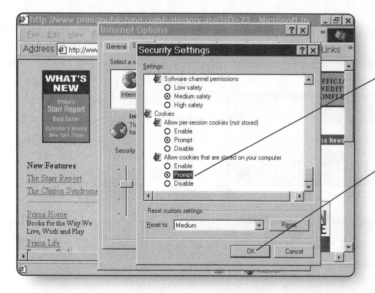

5. Scroll down the **list** until you find the Cookies category.

6. Click on the **option button** that corresponds to how you want to handle cookies. The option will be selected.

7. Click on **OK**. The Internet Options dialog box will appear.

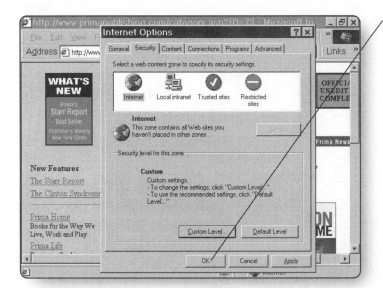

8. **Click** on **OK** to apply your new cookie settings.

DISABLING MULTIMEDIA ELEMENTS FOR FASTER DOWNLOADING

There may be some types of content (such as sound and video files) that you don't want downloaded to your computer while you're surfing the Internet. Multimedia elements typically require significantly more time to download. If you don't want to wait for these files, you can turn them off. Don't worry, you can choose to view these files later when the Web page is displayed in the browser.

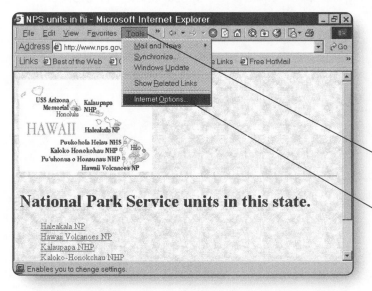

1. **Click** on **Tools**. The Tools menu will appear.

2. **Click** on **Internet Options**. The Internet Options dialog box will appear.

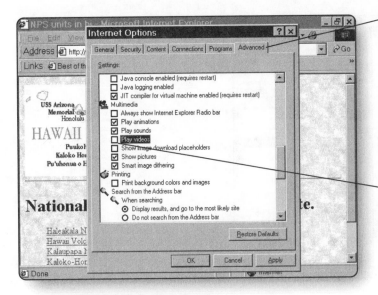

3. **Click** on the **Advanced tab**. The Advanced tab will come to the top of the stack.

4. **Scroll** down to the **Multimedia section** and the list of potential multimedia elements.

5. **Click** on those multimedia **elements** that you do not want displayed in the browser. The check box next to the item will be cleared.

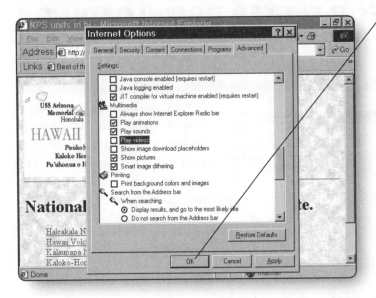

6. **Click** on **OK**. The next time you visit a Web page containing multimedia elements that you have disabled, they will not appear in the Web browser window. You'll notice a blank box on the Web page that contains a red X in the corner. This is the placeholder for the element.

TIP

To display a multimedia element that you have disabled on a Web page, right click on the element's placeholder box and select the Show (multimedia element) command.

9 Playing with Multimedia

If you're looking for entertainment, the Web's full of it. You'll discover music, old time radio broadcasts, movies, and virtual worlds—and that's just the beginning. There are several Internet Explorer components that can enrich your multimedia experience. In this chapter, you'll learn how to:

✦ Play music and video files that you find on the Web

✦ Use Media Player to enjoy multimedia files stored on your computer

✦ Learn to find your way around virtual worlds

ENJOYING WEB ENTERTAINMENT WITH MEDIA PLAYER

Media Player is the component of choice to play a variety of music and video found on the Web. Media Player supports the popular "streaming" format for sound and video, as well as MIDI, MPEG, AVI, RealAudio, RealVideo, Apple Quicktime, and WAV files.

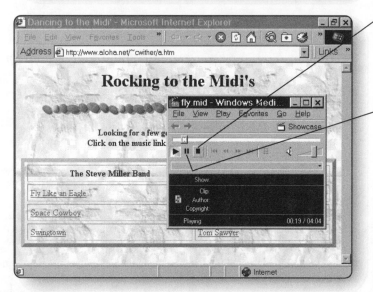

1. **Open** a **Web page** that contains the sound or video file. The Web page will appear in the browser window.

2. **Click** on the **hyperlink** for the sound or video file that you want to play. The Media Player will open. The file will download and begin to play.

3a. **Click** on the **Stop button**. The file will stop playing and return to the beginning.

OR

3b. **Click** on the **Pause button**. The file will stop playing and maintain its position to resume playback.

TIP

Use the Pause button when you want to view a file in short segments.

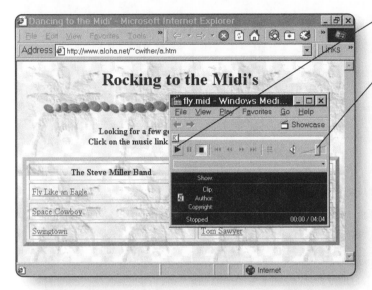

4. Click on the **Play button**. The file will begin playing.

5. **Press** and **hold** the **mouse** button on the Volume Slider and **drag** the **mouse** to the left to reduce the volume or to the right to increase the volume.

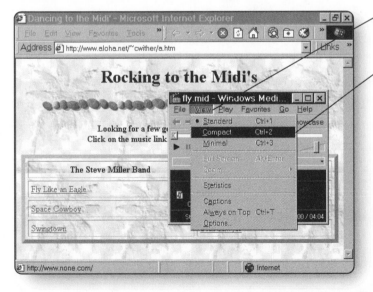

6. Click on **View**. The View menu will appear.

7. Click on one of the **player views**:

✦ **Standard** is the default view. It displays the playback controls, Navigation bar, Seek bar, and Status bar.

✦ **Compact** displays the controls, Seek bar, and Status bar.

✦ **Minimal** takes up the least amount of space. It only displays the controls.

PLAYING MULTIMEDIA FILES STORED ON YOUR COMPUTER

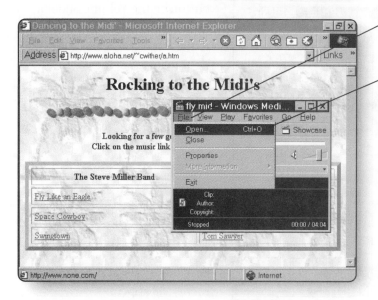

1. Click on **File**. The File menu will appear.

2. Click on **Open** for the Open dialog box.

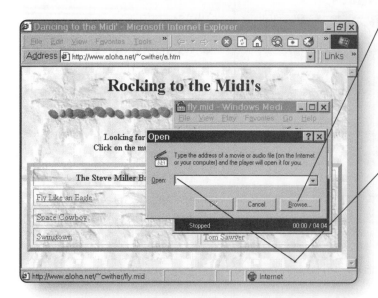

3. Click on **Browse**. The Open dialog box will let you look in your computer's directory for the desired file.

TIP

If you know the location of the file, you can type it in the Open text box. You can also type a URL address in this text box.

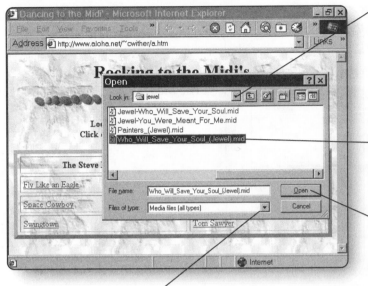

4. **Select** the **folder** that contains the file you want to view. The folder will show in the Look in text box; the files contained within that folder will be listed beneath it.

5. **Click** on the **file** that you want to view. The file name will be selected.

6. **Click** on **Open**. The path and file name will appear in the Open dialog box.

NOTE

If you are looking for files of a certain type, select the type from the Files of type list box.

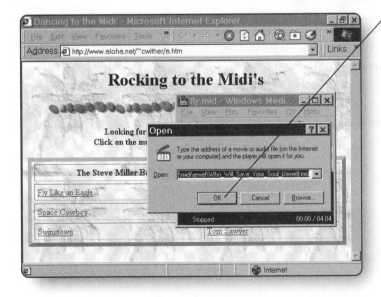

7. **Click** on **OK** to play the file with Media Player.

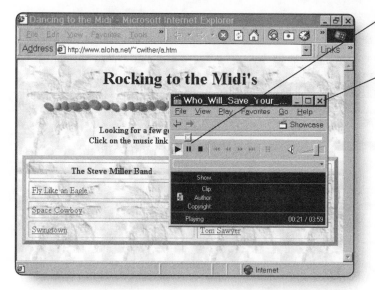

8. Use the **controls** to stop, pause, and start the file.

9. **Click** on the **Close button**. The Media Player will close.

EXPLORING VIRTUAL WORLDS WITH THE VRML PLAYER

VRML (Virtual Reality Markup Language) is the computer technology that simulates real-world, lifelike environments through graphics, sound, and 3-D imagery. VRML is used to create interactive worlds in which you can move around. Virtual Reality allows you to explore the stars and the planets, tour virtual rooms and buildings, and play interactive games.

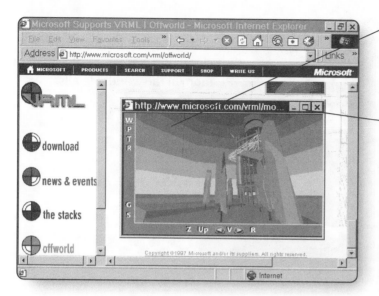

1. Open a **virtual world**. The virtual world may display in the browser window or in the VRML viewer.

2. Click on the **Maximize button** if the virtual world appears in the VRML viewer. The viewer will become larger and provide more viewing area for the virtual world.

> **NOTE**
>
> You can find a number of links to virtual worlds and information about VRML at Microsoft's Web site. Direct your browser to http://www.microsoft.com/vrml/.

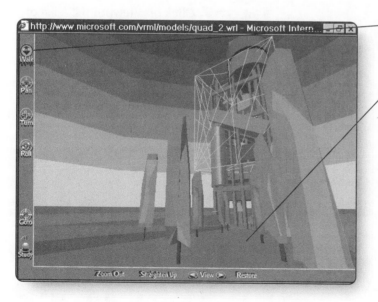

3. Click on the **Walk button**. The cursor will change shape to indicate which tool is selected.

4. Move the **mouse pointer** into the virtual world and **press and hold** the **mouse button**. **Drag** the **mouse** toward the place in the virtual world that you want to see in more detail.

5. **Release** the **mouse button** and the virtual world will come closer and you will be able to see more of the world's details.

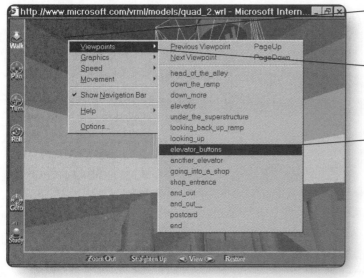

6. **Right-click** on the **virtual world**. A menu will appear.

7. **Click** on **Viewpoints**. A list of places in the virtual world will appear.

8. **Click** on a **place**. The virtual world will move until the place you selected is in view.

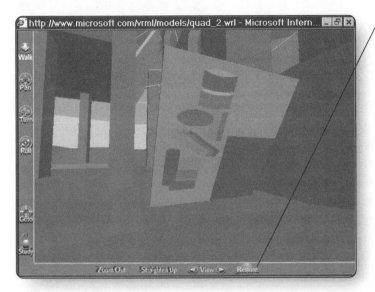

9. **Click** on the **Restore button**. The original view of the virtual world will appear.

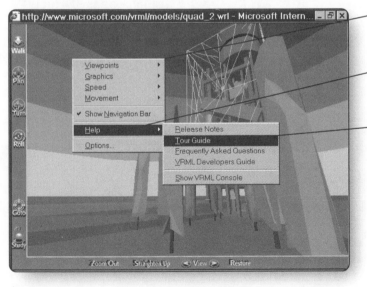

10. **Right-click** on the **virtual world**. A menu will appear.

11. **Click** on **Help**. A list of Help topics will appear.

12. **Click** on a **Help topic** to learn more about how to navigate in virtual worlds. You may want to start with the Tour Guide and Frequently Asked Questions.

PART III REVIEW QUESTIONS

1. What different formats are available to you when saving Web pages? *See "Saving Files" in Chapter 6.*

2. Is it possible to see what a file will look like on paper before it's sent to your printer? *See "Printing Pages" in Chapter 6.*

3. What is the easiest way to add a Web site to your list of Favorites? *See "Getting Started with Favorites" in Chapter 7.*

4. How do you sort your Favorites into folders or groups? *See "Organizing Your List of Favorites" in Chapter 7.*

5. How do you send a selection of your Favorite Web sites in an e-mail message? *See "Sharing Favorites with Your Friends" in Chapter 7.*

6. How do you restrict a Web site from downloading certain elements to your computer? *See "Blocking Content from Harmful Web Sites" in Chapter 8.*

7. Can you keep others from using your computer to access negative Web sites? *See "Preventing Access to Undesirable Web Sites" in Chapter 8.*

8. Is it possible to set up Internet Explorer so that it does not accept cookies? *See "Securing the Cookie Jar" in Chapter 8.*

9. What are the different file types that can be used by the Media Player? *See "Enjoying Web Entertainment with Media Player" in Chapter 9.*

10. Where do you find a shortcut to the different viewpoints found in a virtual world? *See "Exploring Virtual Worlds with the VRML Player" in Chapter 9.*

PART IV

Managing Mail and News With Outlook Express

10 Becoming Familiar with Outlook Express

E-mail is a great way to keep in touch with your family, friends, and business contacts. If you enjoy letter writing, you'll love the instant gratification that e-mail provides. Or, if you just can't get to the post office, e-mail may become an easy way for you to correspond. Before you dive into this e-mail stuff, take some time to become familiar with the Outlook Express screen. In this chapter, you'll learn how to:

✦ Set up e-mail accounts

✦ Receive, read, and delete e-mail messages

✦ Customize the appearance of the Outlook Express screen

✦ Sort and file saved messages

SETTING UP YOUR E-MAIL ACCOUNT

When you first open Outlook Express, a wizard appears to help you set up your e-mail account with an Internet Service Provider (ISP). You will need to go through this setup process before you can send and receive e-mail. If you need help answering the wizard's questions, refer to this chapter along the way.

NOTE

When you set up your Internet account, the ISP assigned you a username and password to access their service. You were also assigned an e-mail address. In addition, the ISP should have given you other access information (either over the phone or in a package that describes how to set up your Internet access). You'll need this information to set up Outlook Express. If you don't have it, contact your ISP.

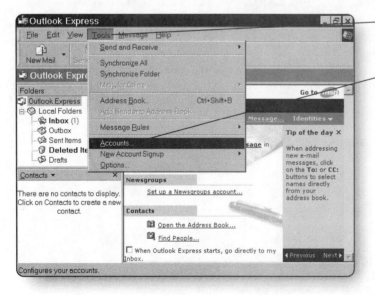

1. Click on **Tools** on the menu bar. The Tools menu will appear.

2. Click on **Accounts**. The Internet Accounts dialog box will open.

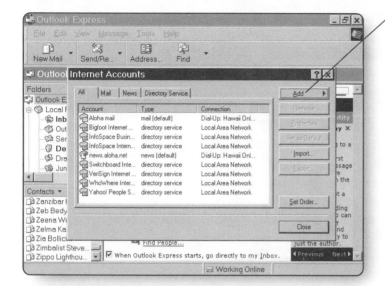

3. Click on **Add**. A shortcut menu will appear.

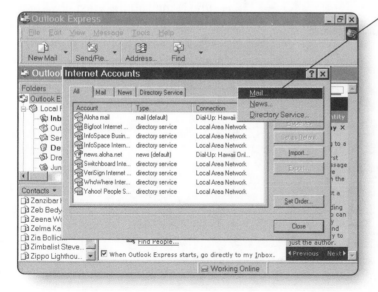

4. Click on **Mail**. The Internet Connection Wizard will start.

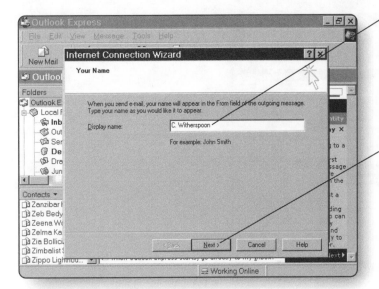

5. **Type** your **name** in the Display name text box. What you type in this box is what will appear in the header information for all your outgoing messages.

6. **Click** on **Next**. The Internet E-mail Address dialog box will appear.

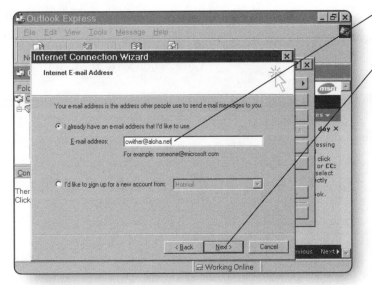

7. **Type** your **e-mail address** in the E-mail address text box.

8. **Click** on **Next**. The E-mail Server Names dialog box will appear.

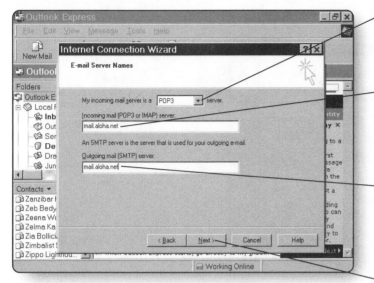

9. Select the e-mail **server** used by your ISP. **Click** on the **down arrow** for a list of servers.

10. Type the name of your ISP's **incoming mail server** in the Incoming mail (POP3 or IMAP) server text box.

11. Type the name of your ISP's **outgoing mail server** in the Outgoing mail (SMTP) server text box.

12. Click on Next. The Internet Mail Logon dialog box will appear.

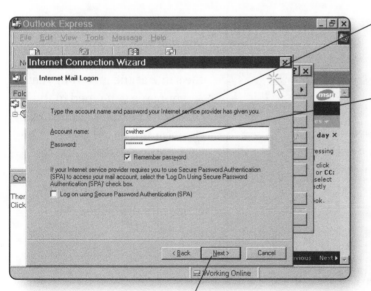

13. Type your **username**, as provided by your ISP, in the POP account name text box.

14. Type your **password**, as provided by your ISP, in the Password text box.

TIP

If you don't want to type your password each time you check your e-mail, place a check in the Remember Password checkbox.

15. Click on Next. The next dialog box will congratulate you.

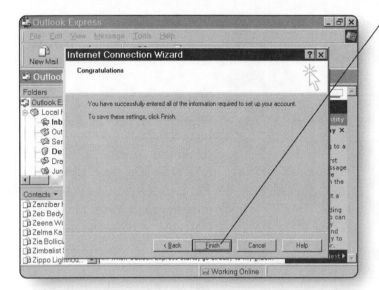

16. Click on Finish. You will be returned to the Internet Accounts dialog box.

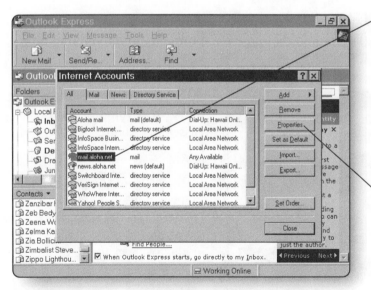

17. Click on the e-mail **account** you just created. The default name given to this account is the same as the incoming mail server name you typed in the E-mail Server Names dialog box of the wizard. The account will be selected.

18. Click on Properties. The Properties dialog box will appear.

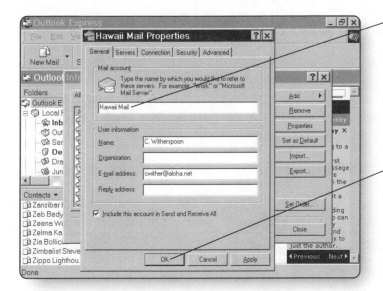

19. Click in the **Mail account text box** and **type** a descriptive **title** for your e-mail account. This window will automatically display the username and e-mail address you specified when setting up your account.

20. Click on **OK**. The Internet Accounts dialog box will appear.

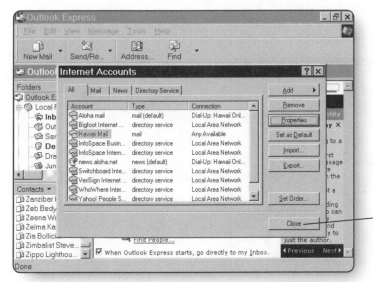

21. Click on **Close**. You are now ready to send and receive e-mail.

CHECKING YOUR E-MAIL

Now that you have your account set up, it's time to go online and check to see if you have any messages waiting for you. Most likely, there will be a welcome letter from your ISP. You might even have a few messages from friends who've been waiting for you to get online!

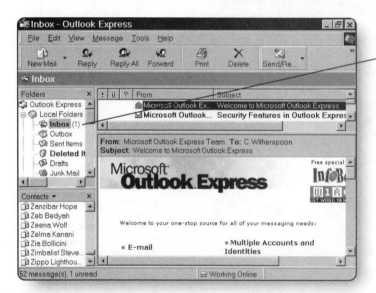

Receiving E-mail

1. **Click** on the **Inbox** folder. The contents of your incoming mailbox will appear.

2. **Click** on the **Send and Receive button**. This will connect you to your ISP; if you have any messages, this will download them to your computer.

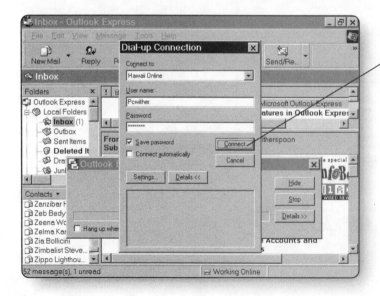

NOTE

If you are not already online, Outlook Express will automatically open a window asking you to connect to your ISP.

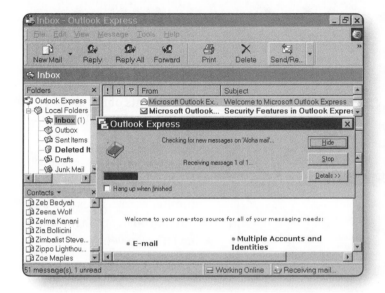

Outlook Express checks your ISP's mail server for new messages and begins the download process.

Take a quick tour around the Outlook Express screen:

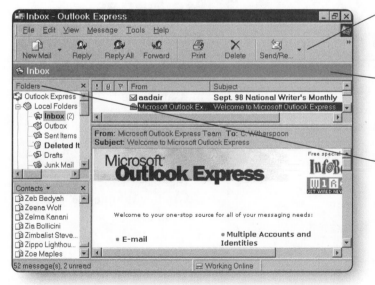

✦ The **Toolbar** contains buttons that execute frequently-used menu commands.

✦ The **Folder Bar** acts as a drop-down list where you can access the various folders in the mail program.

✦ The **Folder List** contains all the folders in the mail program. To view the contents of a folder, click on the folder name.

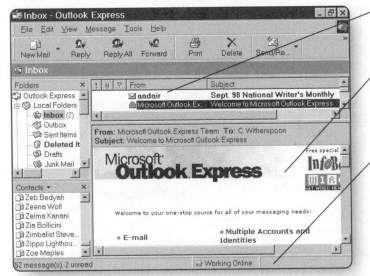

✦ The **Message List** shows all of the messages contained within the selected folder.

✦ The **Preview Pane** displays the contents of the message that is highlighted in the Message List.

✦ The **Status Bar** gives useful information, such as the number of messages you have and how many of them you haven't read yet.

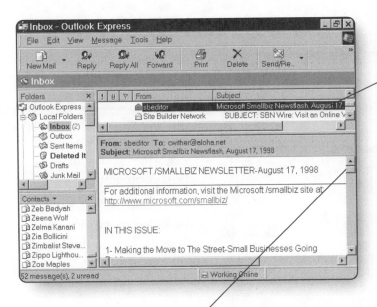

Reading Your Messages

1. Click on the **message** that you want to read. The full message will display in the message pane.

> **TIP**
>
> If you want to display the message in a separate window, double-click on the message.

2. Use the **scrollbars** to browse the list of received messages and to scroll through message contents.

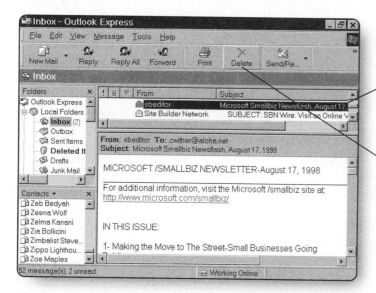

Deleting Messages

1. **Click** on the **message** that you want to delete. The message will be highlighted.

2. **Click** on the **Delete button**. The message will be placed in the Deleted Items folder. The Deleted Items folder works the same way as the Recycle Bin on the Windows desktop. Deleted messages stay in this folder until you permanently remove them from the mail program.

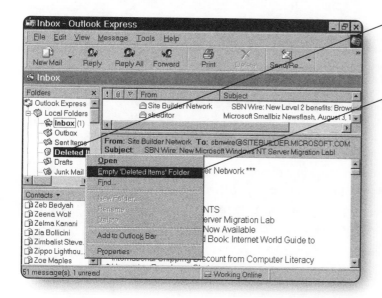

3. **Right-click** on the **Deleted Items folder**. A menu will appear.

4. **Click** on **Empty 'Deleted Items' Folder**. A confirmation dialog box will open.

TIP

If you don't want to remove all the messages from the Deleted Items folder, open the folder, select the messages you want to delete, and press the Delete button.

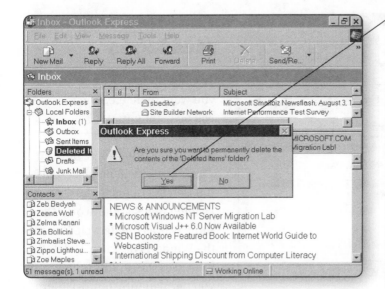

5. Click on **Yes**. All selected files will be removed from the Deleted Items folder.

TIP

You can configure Outlook Express so that it empties the Deleted Items folder each time you close the program. Click on the Tools menu and select Options. On the Maintenance tab, place a check mark next to Empty messages from the Deleted Items folder on exit.

CUSTOMIZING THE OUTLOOK EXPRESS WINDOW

It is possible to reorganize the Outlook Express screen. You may find it more comfortable to work with the Toolbar or Preview Pane in a different location. If you want to scan a list of messages, you can make the Message List window larger. For frequent tasks, save yourself a few mouse clicks by adding a button to the Toolbar instead of using a menu.

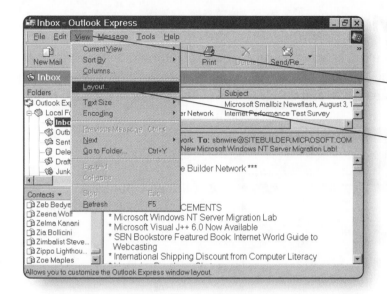

Rearranging the Window

1. **Click** on **View**. The View menu will appear.

2. **Click** on **Layout**. The Window Layout Properties dialog box will open.

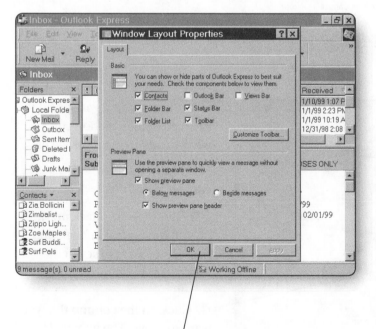

3. **Select or deselect options** to remove or rearrange the different parts of the Outlook Express screen.

TIP

To preview your changes before you close the Options dialog box, select the options and click on the Apply button. You'll see what your preferences look like. If you aren't satisfied, change the options and click on the Apply button again.

4. **Click** on **OK**. The screen will be rearranged using your preferences.

Viewing Message Headers

You can choose how much message information to display in the Message List. Take a look at the types of information you can display and decide what would be the most useful to you.

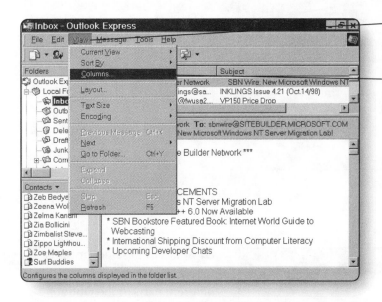

1. **Click** on **View**. The View menu will appear.

2. **Click** on **Columns**. The Columns dialog box will appear.

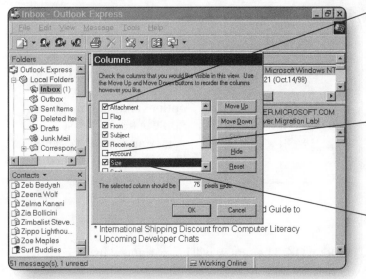

3a. **Place** a **check mark** next to the type of information you want to add to the message list columns.

OR

3b. **Remove** the **check mark** next to the type of information you do not want to see in the message list columns.

4. **Click** on the **column** that you want to move. The item will be selected.

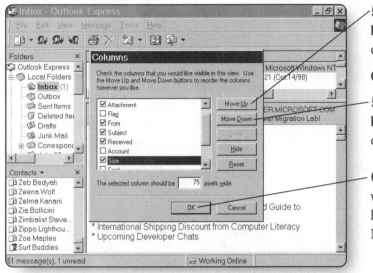

5a. Click on the **Move Up button**. The item will be moved one column to the left.

OR

5b. Click on the **Move Down button**. The item will be moved one column to the right.

6. Click on **OK**. The dialog box will close and the column headings you chose for the Message List will be applied.

Adding Buttons to the Toolbar

There are additional button commands that you can attach to the Outlook Express toolbar. In the last section of this chapter, you'll learn how to file your messages into folders. There's a button that can be added to the toolbar to speed this task. Look through the list of buttons to find commands you'll wish to use frequently.

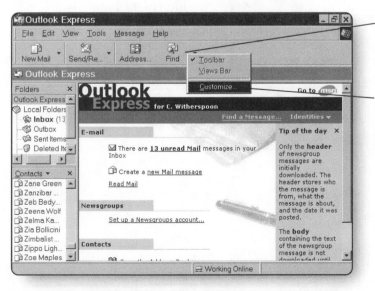

1. **Right-click** on an empty area of the **toolbar**. A menu will open.

2. Click on **Customize**. The Customize Toolbar dialog box will appear.

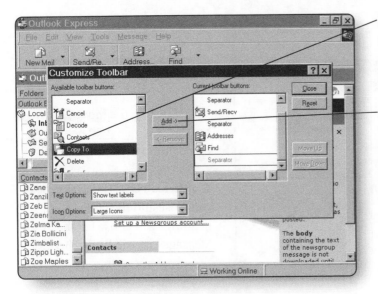

3. **Scroll** through the **Available toolbar buttons list** and **click** on a **button**. The button will be selected.

4. **Click** on **Add**. The button will be added to the Current toolbar buttons list. You can also change the order of the buttons on the toolbar.

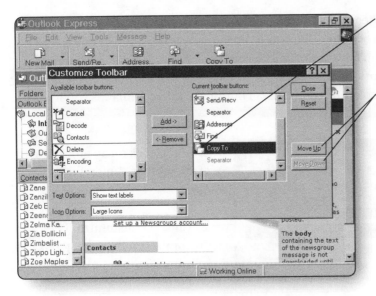

5. **Click** on the **button** that you want to move. The button will be selected.

6. **Click** on the **Move Up or Move Down button**. The position of the button will be moved in the list.

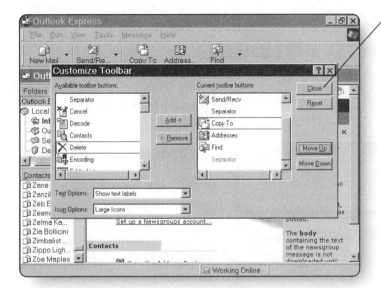

7. Click on Close.

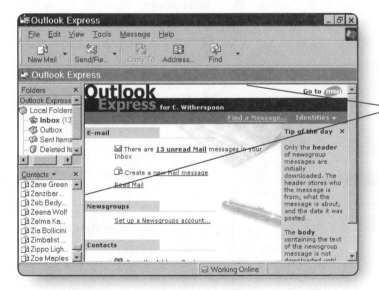

The toolbar will be remodeled to match your changes.

TIP

The size of the Folder List, Message List, and Preview Pane windows can be changed. Click and hold on the border between two frames and drag the mouse pointer until the windows are the desired size. Release the mouse button.

SORTING MESSAGES INTO FOLDERS

After you start accumulating e-mail messages, you may find it inconvenient to keep all of them in the Inbox folder.

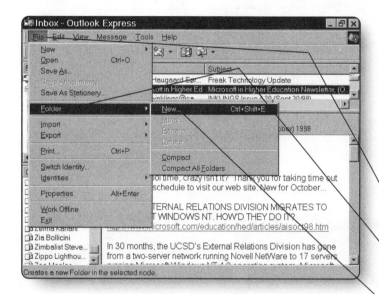

Creating Folders

When your Inbox and Outbox contain so many messages that keeping track of them is distressing, you can create additional folders in which to file your messages.

1. Click on **File**. The File menu will appear.

2. Click on **Folder**. A drop-down menu will appear.

3. Click on **New**. The Create Folder dialog box will open.

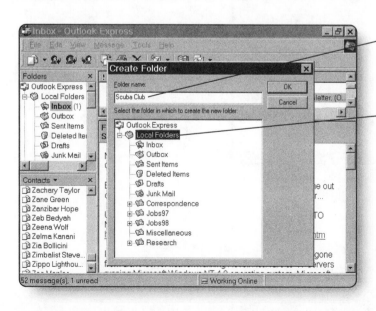

4. Type a **name** for the new folder in the Folder name text box.

5. Click on the **folder** into which you want to place the subfolder. The folder will be selected.

6. Click on **OK**. The list of Outlook Express folders will include your new folder.

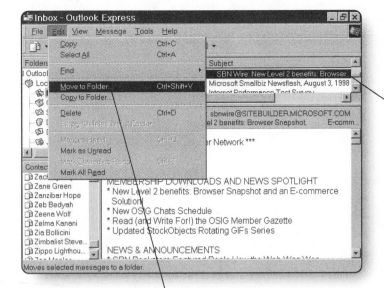

Moving Messages into Folders

1. Click on the **message** that you want to move. The message will be highlighted.

2. Click on **Edit**. The Edit menu will appear.

3. Click on **Move to Folder**. The Move dialog box will open.

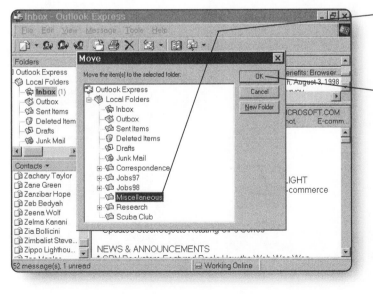

4. Click on the **folder** where you want to store the message. The folder will be selected.

5. Click on **OK**. The message will be moved to the folder you specified.

11 Handling E-mail

It's time to put your letter writing abilities to good use. E-mail is a great way to keep in touch with a next door neighbor, find long lost cousins and start an online reunion, or share text and graphics files with a workgroup. Whatever your reasons for using e-mail, you'll enjoy the ease with which you can keep in contact with people. In this chapter, you'll learn how to:

✦ Send e-mail messages

✦ Attach files to be sent with e-mail messages

✦ Format your messages to look like Web pages

✦ Add the personal touch of stationery to your messages

✦ Filter, route, and file messages

SENDING MESSAGES

Gone are the days of stamps, envelopes, and trips to the post office. Now your letters are delivered to their recipient in just a matter of seconds, and you don't have to make a special trip into town to replenish your stamp supply.

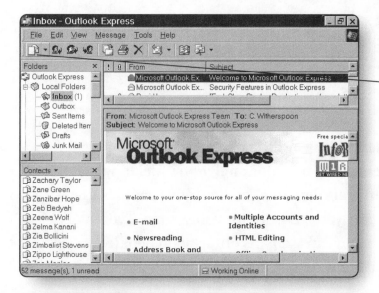

Sending a New Message

1. Click on the **New Message button**. A New Message window will appear.

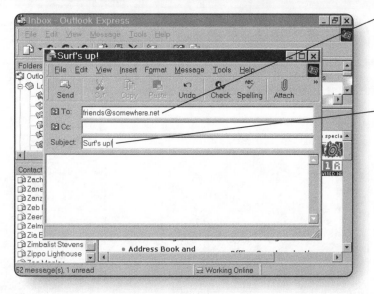

2. Type the **e-mail address** of the person to whom you want to send a message on the To line in the message header box.

3. Type a **subject** for your message in the Subject area.

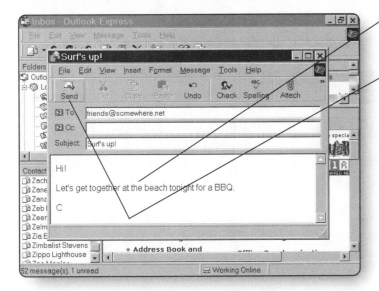

4. **Type** your **message** in the message pane.

5. **Click** on the **Send button**. A dialog box will appear, telling you that your message will be placed in the Outbox.

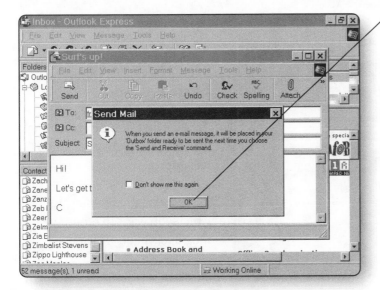

6. **Click** on **OK**. Your Message will be ready to send.

7. **Click** on the **Outbox icon**. Messages waiting to be sent will be itemized in the Message List window.

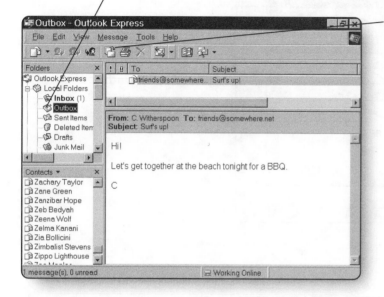

8. **Click** on the **Send and Receive button**. You will be connected to your ISP and your message will be sent to the designated e-mail address.

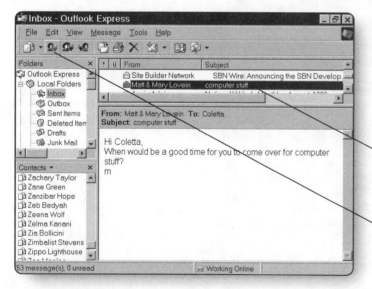

Replying to a Message

1. **Click** on the **Inbox icon**. The list of messages in your inbox will appear.

2. **Click** on the **message** to which you want to reply. The message will be selected.

3. **Click** on the **Reply button**. A message window will display the address, subject, and original message.

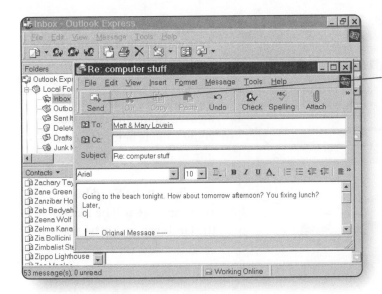

4. **Type** your **reply** in the message pane.

5. **Click** on the **Send button**. Your message will be placed in the Outbox and will be ready to send the next time you connect to your ISP.

Forwarding a Message

1. **Click** on the **Inbox icon**. Your list of received messages will appear.

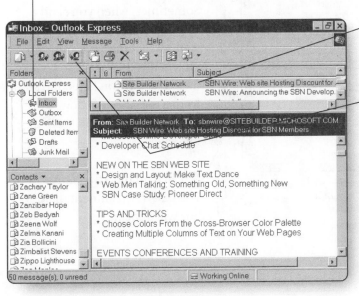

2. **Click** on the **message** that you want to forward. The message will be selected.

3. **Click** on the **Forward Message button**. A message window will show the subject and content of the original message.

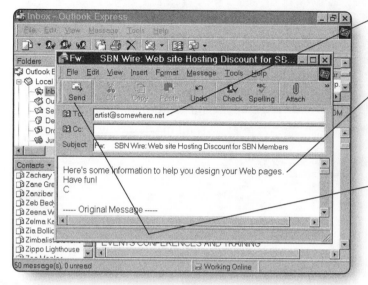

4. Type the **e-mail address** of the recipient in the To area of the header box.

5. Type a **message** in the message pane to let the person know what is being forwarded to him or her.

6. Click on the **Send button**. Your message will be placed in the Outbox and will be ready to send the next time you connect to your ISP.

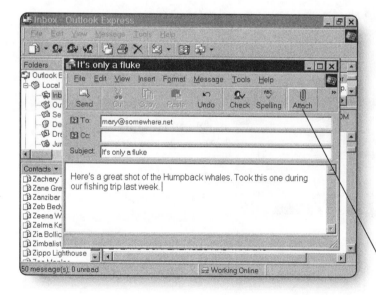

SENDING ATTACHMENTS

Sometimes, when you send a message to someone, you will want to include a file. You can attach any kind of file to your message, but you'll need to start from a message window. You can attach files to any outgoing messages.

1. Click on the **Attach button**. The Insert Attachment dialog box will appear.

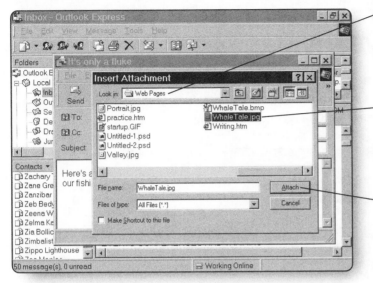

2. In the **Look in** box, **locate** the **directory** where the file to be attached is stored. A list of files will appear.

3. Click on the **file** that you want to attach to your message. The file name will appear in the File name text box.

4. Click on **Attach**.

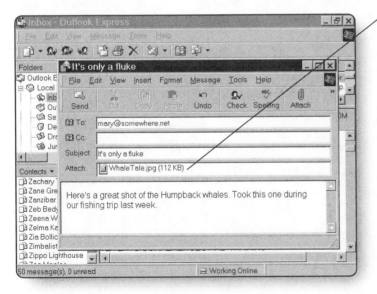

An Attach line will be added in the message header and will show the name of the attached file.

FORMATTING YOUR MESSAGE

One of the newest additions to e-mail is the ability to add HTML formatting to messages. Now you can make your e-mail message look just like a Web page.

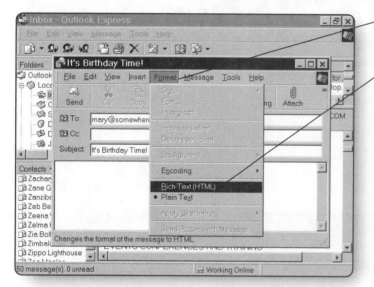

1. Click on Format. The Format menu will appear.

2. Click on Rich Text (HTML). An HTML-formatting toolbar will be added to the new message window.

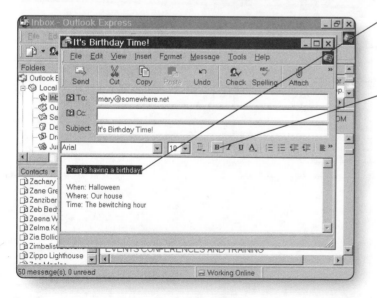

3. Select the text that you want to format. The text will be highlighted.

4. Click on the Bold button. The text will be bolded.

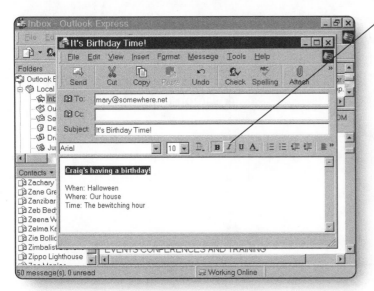

5. **Click** on the **Italic button**. The text will be italicized.

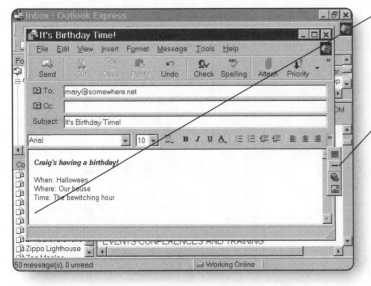

6. **Click** on an empty **space** within the message where you want to add a horizontal line. The Insertion point will move to the spot where you clicked.

7. **Click** on the **Insert Horizontal Line button**. A line will be added to your message. You can use horizontal lines to break your text into sections or to emphasize text headings.

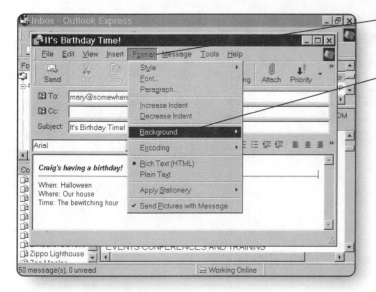

8. **Click** on **Format**. The Format menu will open.

9. **Click** on **Background**. A drop-down menu will appear.

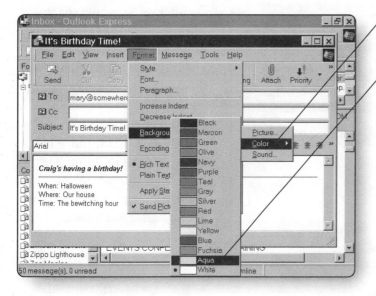

10. **Click** on **Color** for a list of color choices.

11. **Click** on a **color**. The selected color will fill the background of your message.

NOTE

To learn more about formatting Web pages, see Chapter 19, "Getting a Quick Start with FrontPage Express," and Chapter 20, "Making Your Web Pages Look Good."

CHOOSING A STATIONERY

Stationery adds a unique look to all of your correspondence. Outlook Express comes with a number of pre-designed stationeries that cover a range of looks and occassions.

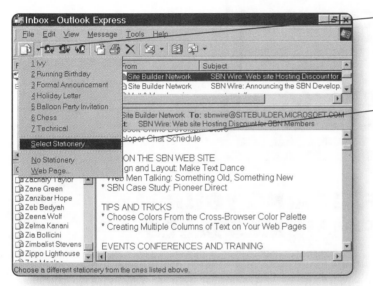

1. **Click** on the **down arrow** to the right of the New Message button on the toolbar. A menu will appear.

2. **Click** on **Select Stationery**. The Select Stationery dialog box will open.

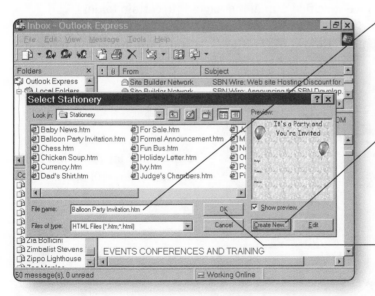

3. **Click** on the **stationery** you want to use. The stationery will be selected.

NOTE

If you want to create your own stationery, click on the Create New button. The Stationery Wizard will walk you through the steps.

4. **Click** on **OK**. A New Message window will open with the selected stationery.

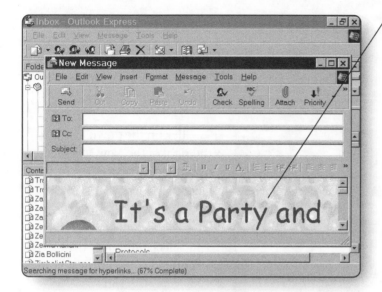

5. **Complete** the **message** and send it.

FILTERING YOUR E-MAIL MESSAGES

Outlook Express contains a Message Rules feature to help automate and organize your e-mail. To automate some routine file management tasks, configure Outlook Express to move specified e-mail messages into certain folders.

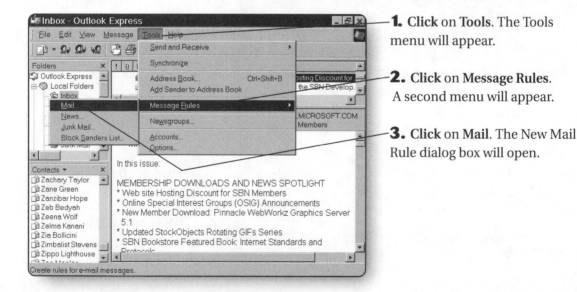

1. **Click** on **Tools**. The Tools menu will appear.

2. **Click** on **Message Rules**. A second menu will appear.

3. **Click** on **Mail**. The New Mail Rule dialog box will open.

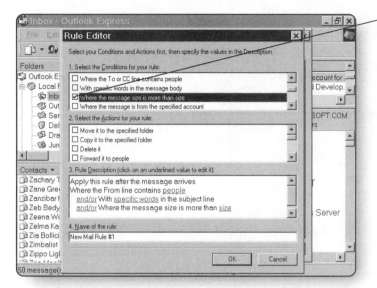

4. **Click** in a **Select the Conditions for your rule check box**. The condition you choose will be selected.

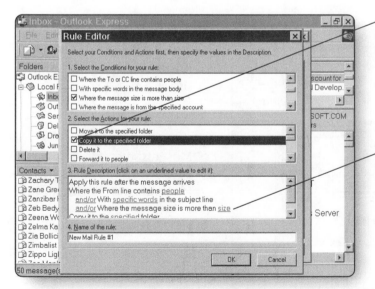

5. **Click** in a **Select the Actions for your rule check box**. This will specify what you want done with any message that fits the Conditions of the rule you are creating.

6. **Click** on the **blue, underlined text** in the Rule Description list. A variety of dialog boxes will open to allow you to input specific rule parameters. Here are a few of the dialog boxes you may see:

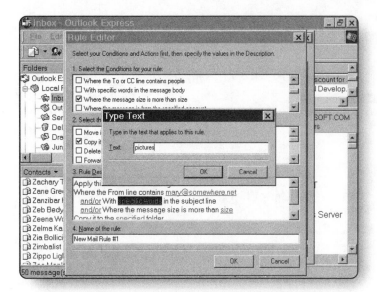

✦ **Type Text** allows you to search for specific words within messages.

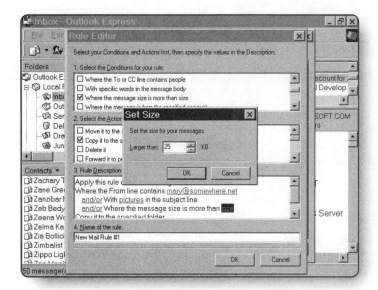

✦ **Set Size** is where you enter a size (in kilobytes) for which the message rule should search.

NOTE

Most text messages will be between 5 and 50 kilobytes (depending on the length of the message).

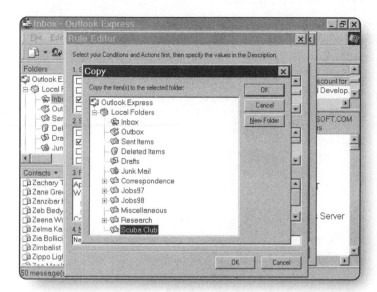

✦ **Copy** allows you to select a folder into which messages will be placed.

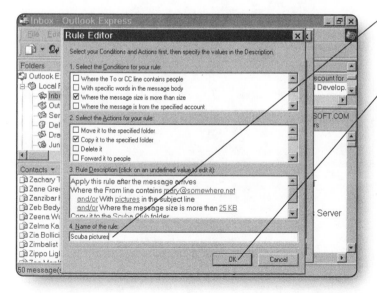

7. Click in the **Name of the rule: text box** and **type** a **name** for the rule.

8. **Click** on **OK** in the Rule Editor window. The Message Rules dialog box will open.

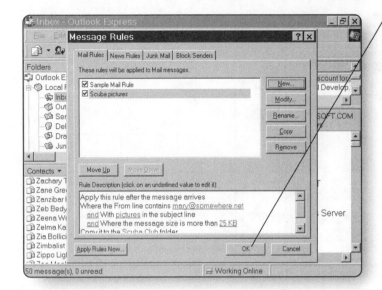

9. Click on **OK**. The next time an arriving message meets your criteria, Outlook Express will perform the action you specified.

12 Working with the Address Book

Windows Address Book is the electronic equivalent of the card file that you keep on your desk or the little black book you keep in your wallet. Windows Address Book works with Outlook Express and makes your life easier by remembering all those e-mail addresses, as well as any information you specify. In this chapter, you'll learn how to:

✦ Create a list of personal contacts with Windows Address Book

✦ Group your contacts to make mass mailings easier

✦ Send mail using your address book

✦ Print the contents of your address book

✦ Locate people and their e-mail addresses on the Internet

CREATING A LIST OF CONTACTS

Use Windows Address Book to keep track of your contacts and communicate with them easily. Taking the time now to learn about Address Book's features will make the job of maintaining contacts with individuals and groups a snap.

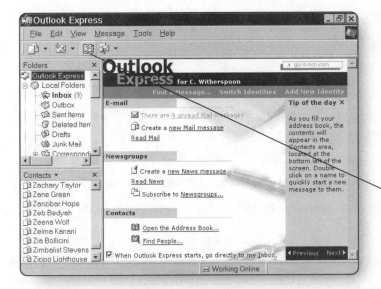

Adding a New Contact

Adding new names to your address book is as simple as clicking on a few buttons and typing information into a dialog box.

1. Click on the **Address Book icon**. The Address Book will appear.

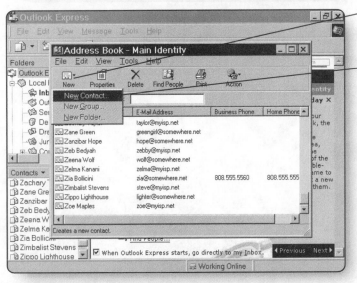

2. Click on the **New button**. A cascading menu will appear.

3. Click on **New Contact**. The Properties dialog box will open and the Name tab will be at the top of the stack.

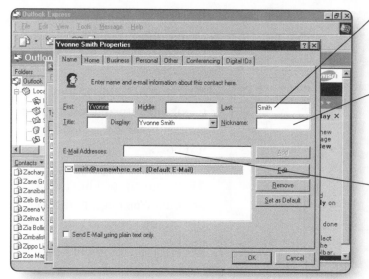

4. Type the full **name** of your contact in the First, Middle, and Last text boxes.

5. Type a **nickname** for your contact in the Nickname text box. Use a name that is easy for you to remember.

6. Type the **e-mail address** for your contact in the Add new text box.

7. Click on **Add**. Your contact's e-mail address will be added to your address book when you accept the changes and close the Properties dialog box.

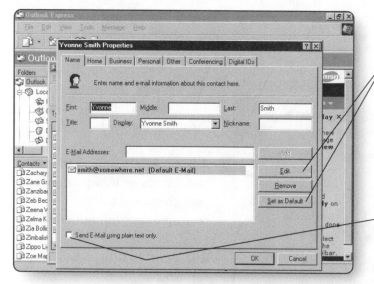

8. Click on **Send E-Mail using plain text only** if your contact uses a mail program that does not read HTML-formatted messages. A check mark will appear in the box.

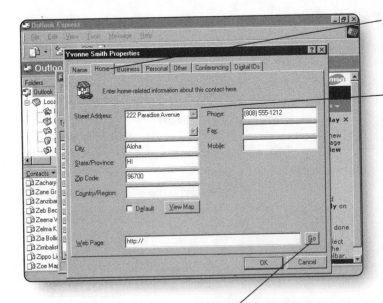

9. **Click** on the **Home tab**. The Home tab will come to the top of the stack.

10. **Type** the **address and telephone information** for your contact in the corresponding text boxes.

11. If your contact has a personal Web page, **type** that **URL** in the Personal Web Page text box.

NOTE

If you are connected to the Internet, click on the Go button to visit your contact's Web page. Internet Explorer will open and the browser window will display the Web page. You can also click on the View Map button to see where they live.

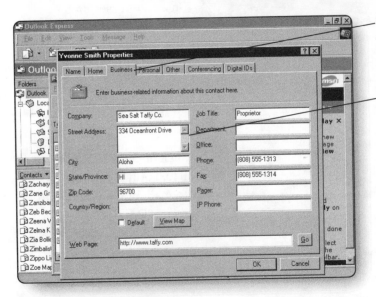

12. **Click** on the **Business tab**. The Business tab will come to the top of the stack.

13. **Type** the **business address and telephone information** for your contact in the corresponding text boxes.

14. **Type** the **URL** of your contact's business Web page in the Business Web Page text box.

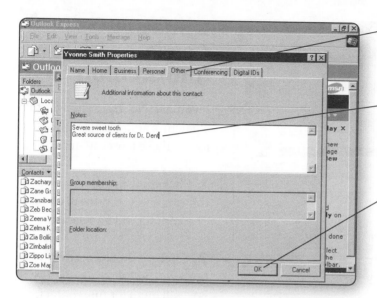

15. **Click** on the **Other tab**. The Other tab will come to the top of the stack.

16. **Type information** in the Notes text box. This is a useful place to keep important facts about your contact.

17. **Click** on **OK**. The Properties dialog box will close and your contact will be added to the Address Book.

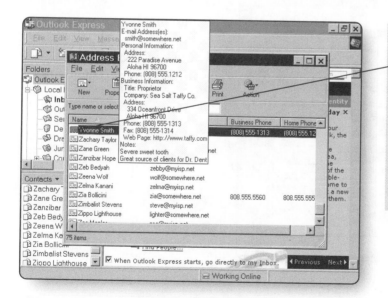

TIP

If you want to see all of the information about a contact but you don't want to open the Properties dialog box, place the mouse pointer over the contact's entry in the Address Book until a screen tip appears.

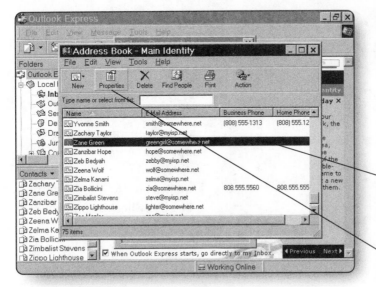

Updating Contact Information

If you need to make changes to a person's address listing, just follow these few easy steps.

1. Click on the **contact** whose information you want to change. The contact will be selected.

2. Click on the **Properties button**. The Properties dialog box will open for this contact.

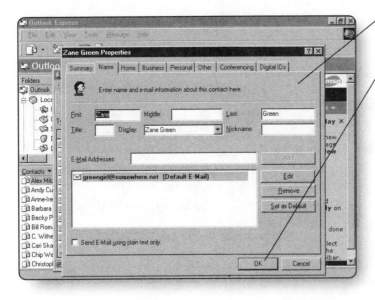

3. Make the necessary **changes** or **additions**.

4. Click on **OK**. The address listing will be updated.

FORMING GROUPS

In many cases, you will find that organizing your contacts into groups by job, organization, interest, or some other characteristic is a great help. Mailing lists can be managed much more easily this way.

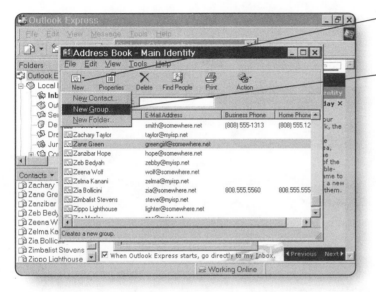

1. Click on the New button. A cascading menu will appear.

2. Click on New Group. The Properties dialog box will open.

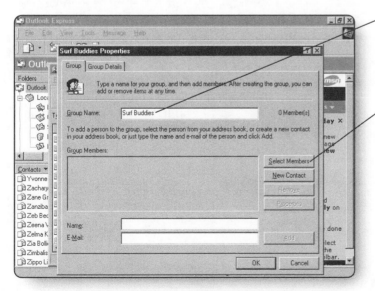

3. Type a name in the Group Name text box. Use a name that describes the group or its function.

4. Click on the Select Members button. The Select Group Members dialog box will appear.

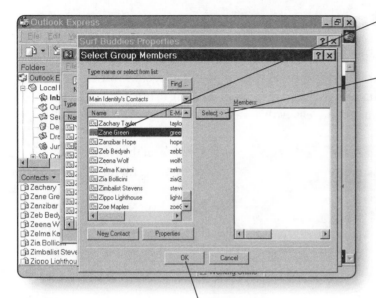

5. Click on the **name** of a contact in the Name list.

6. Click on **Select**. This contact's name will be added to the Members list.

7. Choose additional names and select them for the list. These names will be added to the Members list. When you send e-mail to the group, copies will be sent to the e-mail address of each contact on the Members list.

8. Click on **OK**. You will be returned to the Group Properties dialog box.

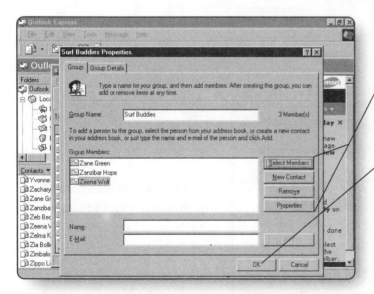

NOTE

Use the New Contact, Select Members, Remove, and Properties buttons to manage your group list.

9. Click on **OK**. The group will be added to your address book.

SENDING MAIL FROM THE ADDRESS BOOK

You can send mail directly from your address book.

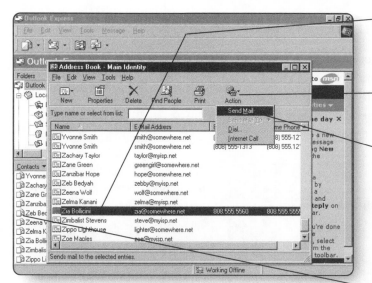

1. **Select** a **contact** to whom you want to send an e-mail message. The entry will be selected.

2. **Click** on the **Action button**. A drop-down menu will appear.

3. **Click** on **Send Mail**. A new message window will open. The contact's address will already be entered on the To line in the message header.

TIP

If you have the Contact List displayed below the Folder list in the Outlook Express window, you can send mail to a contact by double-clicking on the contact's name in the list.

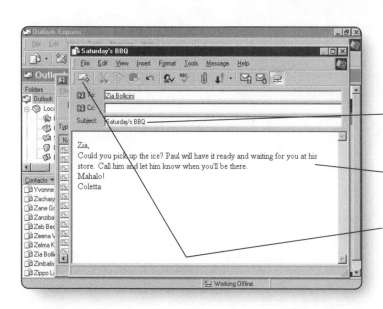

4. **Type** a **subject** for your message in the Subject area.

5. **Type** your **message** in the message area.

6. **Click** on the **Send button**. Your message will be placed in the Outbox until you connect to the Internet and send the message.

NOTE

To learn more about sending messages, refer to Chapter 11, "Handling E-mail."

PRINTING AN ADDRESS LIST

Occasionally, having a hard copy of your address list is helpful. You can use the printed list as a permanent file copy or bring it with you when you are away from your computer. This can be useful when you are traveling or working from a desk other than your own.

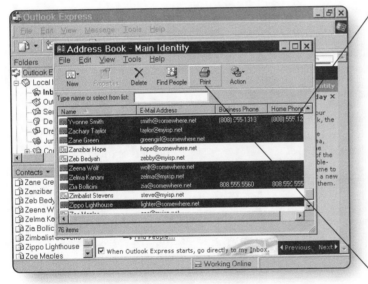

1. Select the contacts you want to include in a printed address listing. The contacts will be selected.

NOTE

You can select more than one contact at a time by pressing the Ctrl key and clicking on each contact name.

2. Click on the Print button. The Print dialog box will appear.

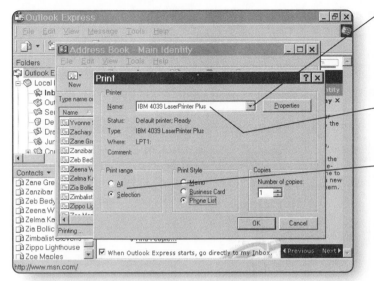

3. Click on the **down arrow** next to the Name list box. A drop-down menu of available printers will open.

4. Click on a **printer** from the list. The printer will be selected.

5. Click on the Print range option **All** to print the entire address book or **Selection** to print only those contact names that were highlighted. The option will be selected.

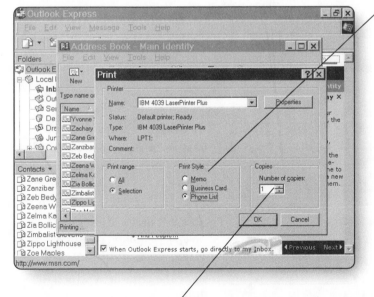

6. Click on one of the following **Print Style options** for your address listing printout:

✦ **Memo** style prints all the information in the address book.

✦ **Business Card** style prints only information that you would normally see on a business card.

✦ **Phone List** style prints only names and phone numbers.

7. Click on the **up** and **down arrows** to select the number of copies you want printed.

8. Click on **OK**. Your address list will begin to print.

SEARCHING FOR PEOPLE

You can search for e-mail addresses online by using a number of directory services and Internet search tools. These directory services work much like your local phone book, but they are not limited to local area listings.

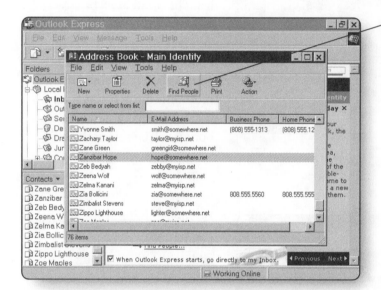

1. **Click** on the **Find People button**. The Find People dialog box will appear.

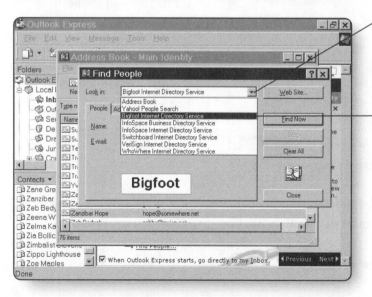

2. **Click** on the **down arrow** next to the Look in list box. A list of available directory services will appear.

3. **Click** on the **directory service** that you want to use. The dialog box will change to show the criteria by which the directory service allows you to search.

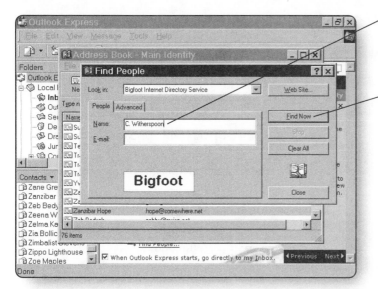

4. **Type** the **name** of the person you want to find in the Name text box.

5. **Click** on **Find Now**. The directory service looks for any matches to your search query.

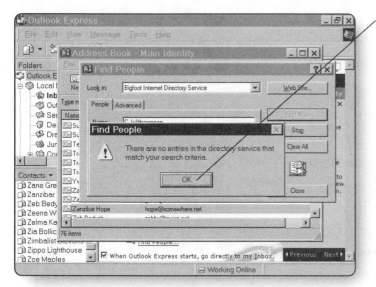

6. **Click** on **OK** if a dialog box opens letting you know that no matches were found. The Find People dialog box will return.

NOTE

You may need to select a different directory service if you aren't having any luck locating someone.

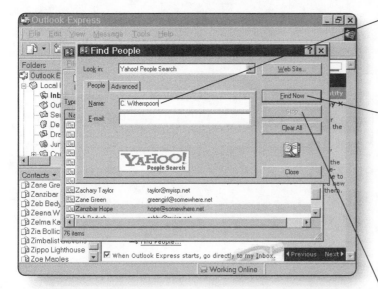

7. Retype the **name** of the person you want to find in a slightly different way to attempt better search results.

8. **Click** on **Find Now**. A dialog box will appear asking you to wait until the directory service finishes its search. When the directory service completes the search, it will list the results at the bottom of the Find People dialog box.

NOTE

Click on Stop if you don't want to wait while the directory service compiles the search results.

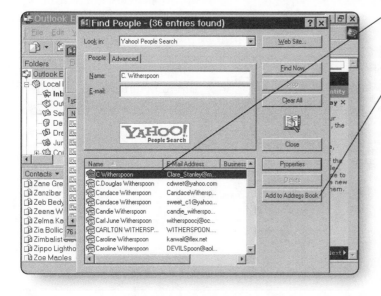

9. **Click** on the **name** of the person you are seeking. The name will be selected.

10. **Click** on **Add to Address Book**. The person's e-mail address will be added to your Windows Address Book. You can now send him or her e-mail directly from your address book.

11. **Click** on **Close** when you are finished with your search. The Find People dialog box will close.

13 Using News

Finding and joining one of the news "bulletin board" discussion groups on your favorite subject is easier than you think. With thousands of groups from which to choose, there's something on the Internet for everyone. If you want to learn more about computers, check out the myriad computer-related newsgroups. You can usually find someone willing to help you solve a problem, answer a question about how to use a software program, or discuss the future of computers. Newsgroups are a great way to meet people, and Outlook Express can get you connected. In this chapter, you'll learn how to:

✦ Set up a news server to access newsgroups

✦ Subscribe to newsgroups and read, save, and manage messages

✦ Post your own messages to newsgroups

✦ Use filters to limit newsgroup messages

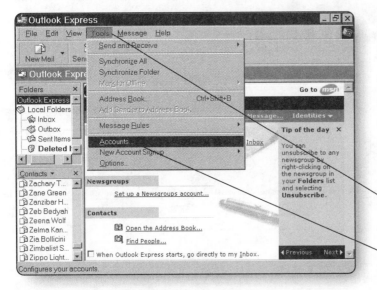

LOCATING A NEWS SERVER

This section will guide you through the process of connecting to your ISP and setting up access to a newsgroup server on your computer.

1. **Click** on **Tools**. The Tools menu will appear.

2. **Click** on **Accounts**. The Internet Accounts dialog box will open.

3. **Click** on **Add**. A menu of options will appear.

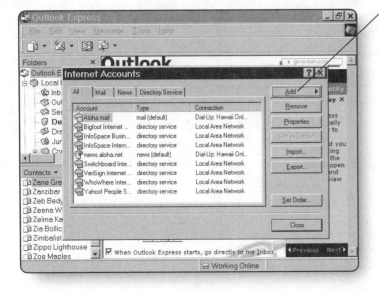

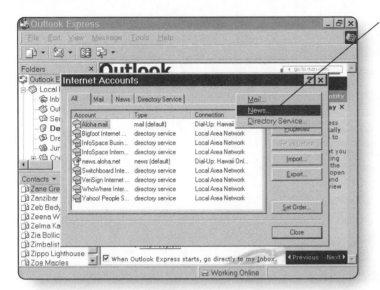

4. Click on **News**. The Internet Connection Wizard will open with the Your Name screen displayed.

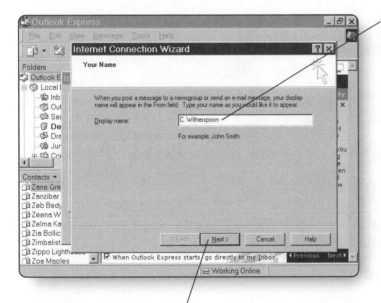

5. Type your **name** in the Display name text box. The way that you type your name here is how you will be identified in all newsgroup discussion threads.

TIP

If you want to maintain some privacy, just use your first name or an alias. That way people won't know your true identity.

6. Click on **Next**. The Internet News E-mail Address screen will appear.

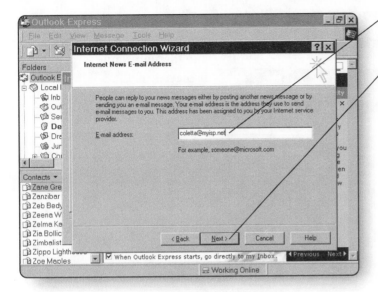

7. Type your **e-mail address** in the E-mail address text box.

8. Click on Next. The Internet News Server Name screen will appear.

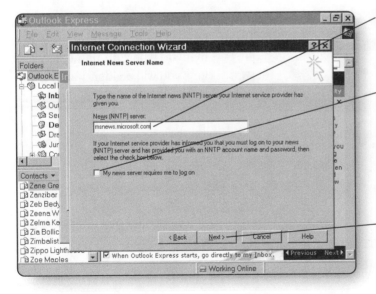

9. Type the address of your ISP's **news server** in the News (NNTP) server text box.

10. Click on **My news server requires me to log on** if your ISP requires a user name and password to access the news server. A check will appear in the box.

11. Click on Next. The Congratulations screen will appear.

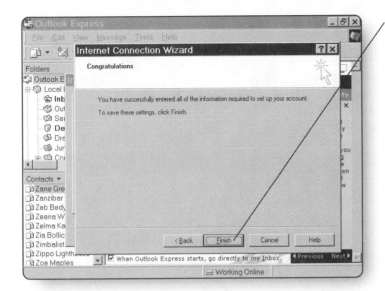

12. **Click** on **Finish**. You will return to the Internet Accounts dialog box.

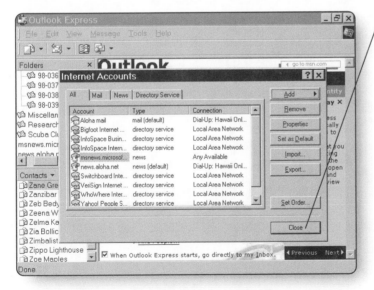

13. **Click** on **Close**. The news server will be added to your list of Internet accounts. Outlook Express will ask you if you'd like to download newsgroups from the server.

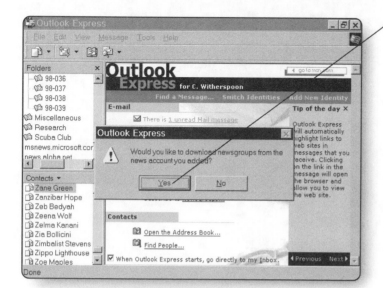

14. Click on **Yes**. Outlook Express will begin downloading a list of available newsgroups.

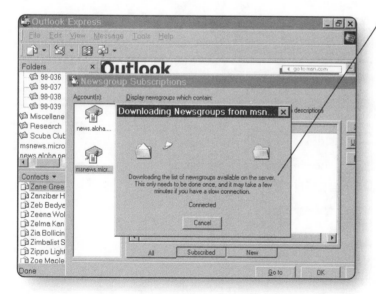

The list of newsgroups will be transferred to your computer.

MAKING THE MOST OF THE NEWS

Before you can participate in newsgroup discussions, you'll need to make the newsgroup messages easy to view and readily available. You can do this by subscribing to the various newsgroups that interest you.

Subscribing to Newsgroups

NOTE

The Newsgroup Subscriptions dialog box will appear after the list of newsgroups has downloaded from your computer. If you don't see this dialog box, open the Tools menu and select Newsgroups.

1. Type a **keyword** that describes the type of newsgroups in which you're interested into the Display newsgroups which contain text box. Newsgroups that contain matching words will appear in the newsgroups list window.

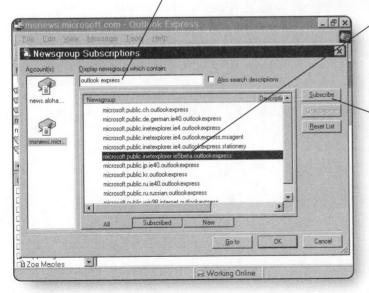

2. Click on the **newsgroup** to which you want to subscribe. The newsgroup will be highlighted.

3. Click on **Subscribe**. A check mark will appear next to a newsgroup's name.

NOTE
The newsgroups to which you subscribe appear in the Folders frame, listed under the news server.

Reading Newsgroup Messages

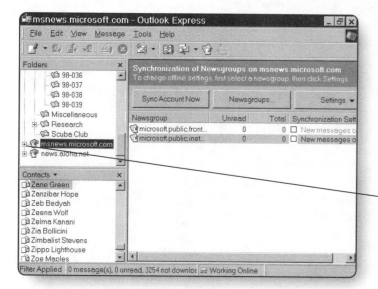

To read the messages in the groups to which you have subscribed, just follow these steps.

1. In the Folders window, **click** the **plus sign** next to the news server to which you want to connect. A list of subscribed newsgroups will display below the highlighted news sever.

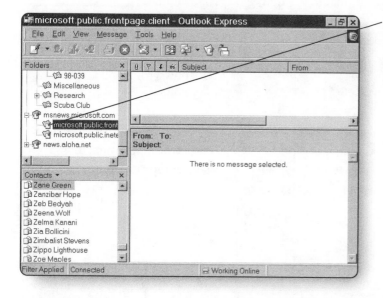

2. **Click** on the name of a subscribed **newsgroup**. The newsgroup headers will start downloading to your computer.

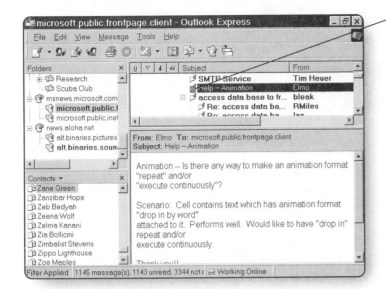

3. Click on the newsgroup **message** that you want to read. The message will open in the preview pane.

Saving Attachments

Newsgroup messages may contain attachments. Attachments are indicated by a paper clip to the right of the header information.

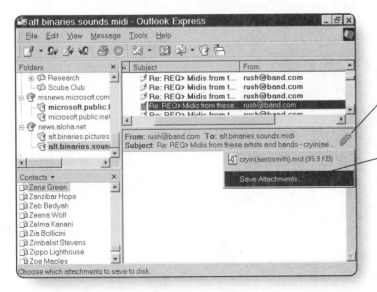

1a. Click on **File**. The File menu will appear.

OR

1b. Click on the **Paper clip icon**. A menu will appear.

2. Click on **Save Attachments**. The Save Attachments dialog box will open with a list of attached files.

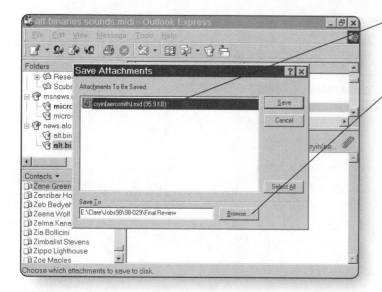

3. Select the **file or files** that you want to save. The files will be highlighted.

4. Click on **Browse**. The Browse for Folder dialog box will appear.

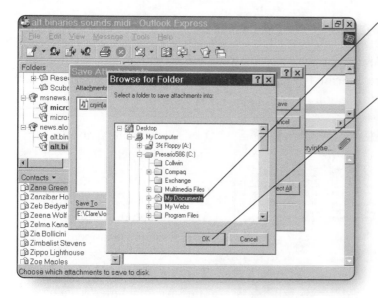

5. Locate and click on the **folder** in which you want to save the file.

6. Click on **OK**. The Save Attachments dialog box will return.

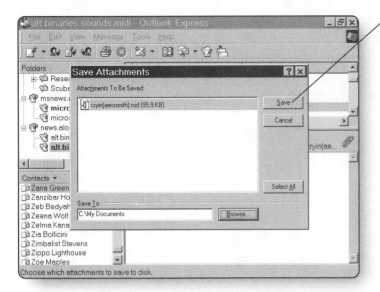

7. Click on **Save**. The attachment will be saved to the location that you specified.

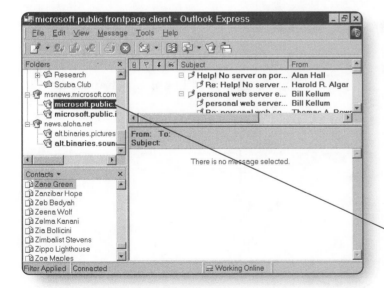

Downloading Newsgroup Messages

If you want to read newsgroup messages but you don't want to do so while you are connected to your ISP, download the messages to your computer to peruse them later.

1. Click on the **newsgroup** that you want to download. The newsgroup headers will appear in the Message List.

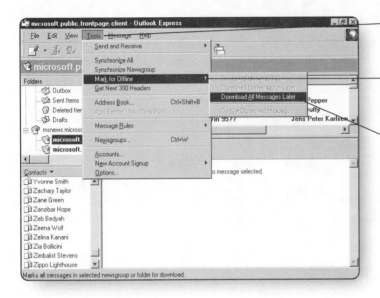

2. Click on **Tools** in the menu bar. The Tools menu will appear.

3. Click on **Mark for Offline**. A second menu will appear.

4. Click on **Download All Messages Later**. A download symbol will appear next to each of the messages in the newsgroup.

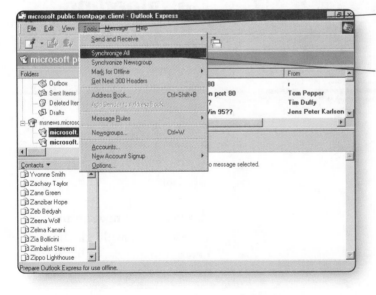

5. Click on **Tools**. The Tools menu will appear.

6. Click on **Synchronize All**.

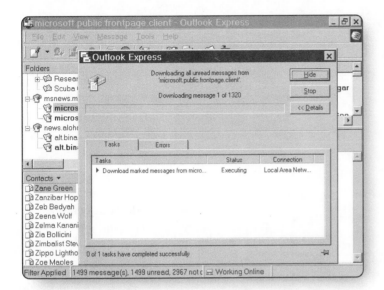

The download progress box will appear. When the messages have finished downloading, you can disconnect from your ISP and read the messages at your leisure.

Automatically Marking Messages as Being Read

You can change how long you have to read a message before it is automatically marked as read. When you change this option, it affects all the newsgroup messages on all of the news servers you have set up in Outlook Express.

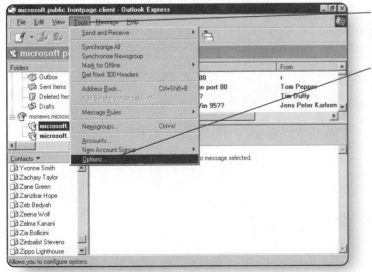

1. **Click** on **Tools**. The Tools menu will appear.

2. **Click** on **Options**. The Options dialog box will open.

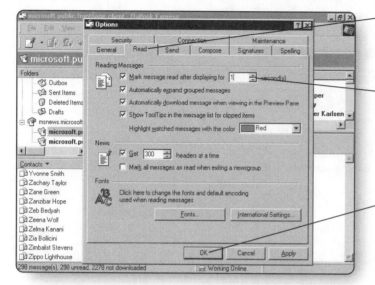

3. Click on the **Read tab**. The tab will come to the top of the stack.

4. Click the **up** and **down arrows** to select the number of seconds of previewing required before a message is marked as read.

5. Click on OK. Your changes will be applied to all newsgroup messages.

TIP

You can add toolbar buttons for the various Mark as Read and Download commands.

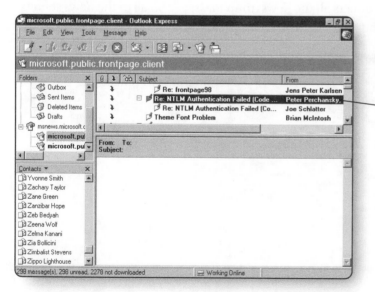

Marking a Thread as Being Read

1. Click on any **message** in a thread. The message will be selected.

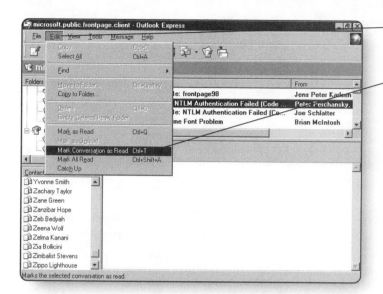

2. **Click** on **Edit**. The Edit menu will appear.

3. **Click** on **Mark Conversion as Read**.

TIP
To mark the entire newsgroup as being read, click on Mark All Read.

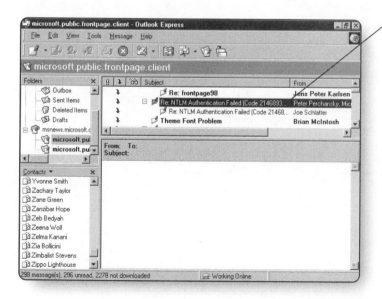

The messages in the selected thread will change from bold type to regular type.

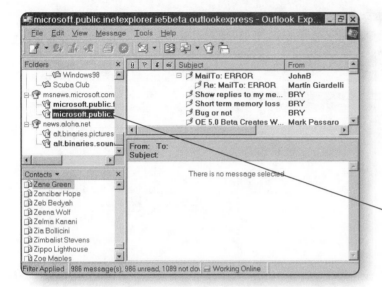

Finding Messages

If you don't want to scroll through lists of newsgroup messages to find the one you need, use this quick search shortcut to find a particular message.

1. Click on the **newsgroup** you want to search. The newsgroup will be selected.

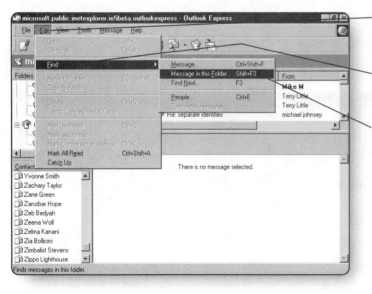

2. Click on **Edit**. The Edit menu will appear.

3. Click on **Find**. A second menu will appear.

4. Click on **Message in this Folder**. The Find dialog box will open.

5. In the Look for: text box, **type keywords** that describe the information for which you are looking.

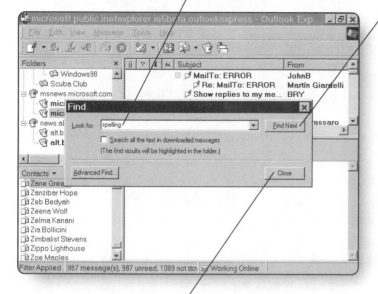

6. Click on the **Find Next button**. Outlook Express will search for the message and will highlight the first message that matches your request in the Message pane and will display the message in the message preview panes.

7. Click on the **Find Next button**. The next message that matches your request will be highlighted in the Message pane and displayed in the preview pane.

8. Click on the **Close button** when you are finished searching through the newsgroups. The Find dialog box will close.

POSTING MESSAGES

Once you become familiar with a newsgroup, you will probably want to post replies to messages posted by other members. Sometimes, you may want to post messages with attachments that you want to send to the group.

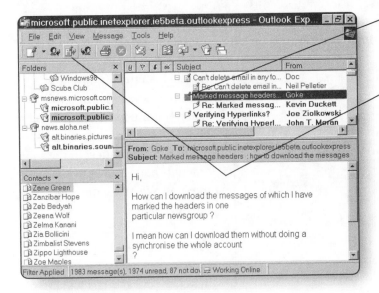

1. Click on the **message** to which you want to respond. The message will be selected.

2. Click on the **Reply to Group button.** A message window will appear with the newsgroup and subject fields filled in and the original message in the message pane.

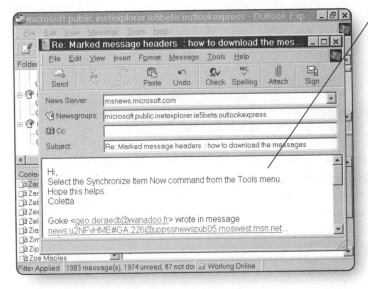

3. Type a **reply message** in the message area.

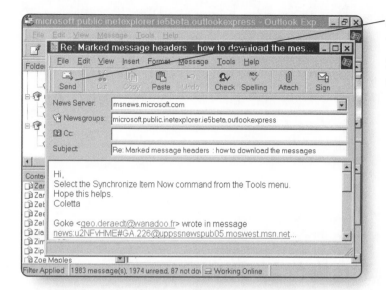

4. **Click** on the **Send button**. The message will be placed in your Outbox, and a Post News dialog box will open.

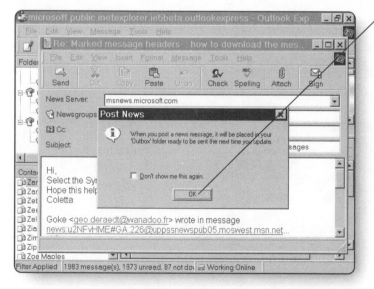

5. **Click** on **OK**. Your message will be sent to the newsgroup for posting.

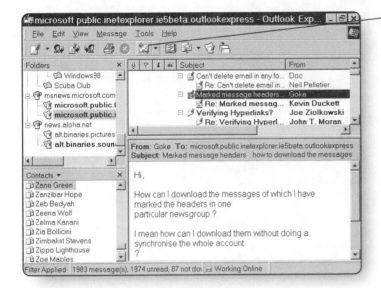

6. Click on the **Send button**.

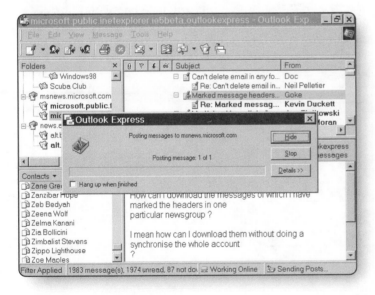

A download dialog box will display status information and your message will be posted to the newsgroup.

NOTE

To see your message, click on the Tools menu and select Get Next Headers.

USING NEWSGROUP FILTERS

Hundreds of messages are posted daily to newsgroups. For this reason, you need to be able to isolate just the ones that interest you. You can easily set criteria for filtering your newsgroups so that you can exclude messages that you don't want to view.

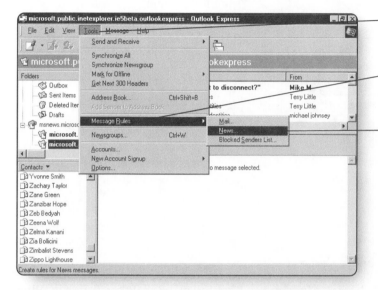

1. Click on **Tools**. The Tools menu will appear.

2. Click on **Message Rules**. A second menu will appear.

3. Click on **News**. The New News Rule dialog box will open.

NOTE

Refer back to Chapter 11, "Handling E-mail," for more help on using Message Rules.

4. Click in a **Select the Conditions for your rule check box**. The condition you choose will be selected.

5. Click in a **Select the Actions for your rule check box**. This will specify what you want done with any message that fits the Conditions of the rule you are creating.

6. Click on the **blue underlined text** in the Rule Description list. A variety of dialog boxes will open to allow you to input specific rule parameters.

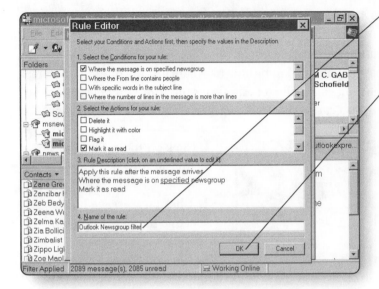

7. Click in the **Name of the rule: text box** and **type** a **name** for the rule.

8. **Click** on **OK** in the Rule Editor window. The Message Rules dialog box will open.

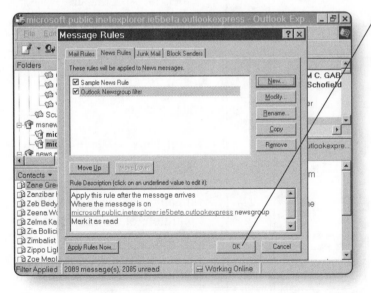

9. **Click** on **OK**. The next time an arriving message meets your criteria, Outlook Express will perform the action you specified.

PART IV REVIEW QUESTIONS

1. What are the different elements of the Outlook Express window? *See "Receiving E-mail" in Chapter 10.*

2. How can you easily manage your e-mail messages? *See "Sorting Messages into Folders" in Chapter 10.*

3. What are the different ways that you can respond to an e-mail message? *See "Sending Messages" in Chapter 11.*

4. What types of files can be sent as attachments to an e-mail message? *See "Sending Attachments" in Chapter 11.*

5. Is it possible to make your e-mail messages look like Web pages? *See "Formatting Your Message" in Chapter 11.*

6. Can a single Address Book entry have more than one e-mail address for a person? *See "Adding a New Contact" in Chapter 12.*

7. How do you set up the Address Book so that one e-mail message can be sent to a number of people? *See "Forming Groups" in Chapter 12.*

8. How do you add a second newsgroup server to Outlook Express? *See "Locating a News Server" in Chapter 13.*

9. How do you set up a list of newsgroups that you want to view regularly? *See "Subscribing to Newsgroups" in Chapter 13.*

10. What feature of Outlook Express allows you to ignore messages that you don't want to see? *See "Using Newsgroup Filters" in Chapter 13.*

PART V

Communicating with Others on the Web

From
☒ aa
🔲 Mi

: Microsoft
ject: Welco

Micros
Out

Welcome to

• E-mail

14 Becoming Familiar with Microsoft Chat

If you enjoy visiting chat rooms, Microsoft Chat can make your visits come alive. Microsoft Chat uses comic book characters that can add animation and expression to your discussions. Microsoft Chat gives you access to thousands of chat rooms. The range of topics you can discuss with friends and strangers is endless. Before you go into "chat" mode, take some time to get familiar with the program. In this chapter, you'll learn how to:

✦ Create a chat room identity

✦ Switch between comic strip and text interfaces

✦ Change the appearance of the Chat window

✦ Save a transcript of a chat session

SETTING UP YOUR IDENTITY

When you open Microsoft Chat, the Microsoft Chat Connection dialog box will open automatically. This dialog box gives you the opportunity to select your starting point and your persona each time you use Microsoft Chat. Your starting point is the first chat room that you want to visit. You always have the opportunity to move to a different room. Your persona is created from the personal information that you choose to make public and the comic character that you use to represent yourself.

> **NOTE**
>
> See Chapter 1, "Starting and Exiting Programs," if you need help starting the program. If Microsoft Chat isn't installed on your computer, see the appendix for help getting and installing the program.

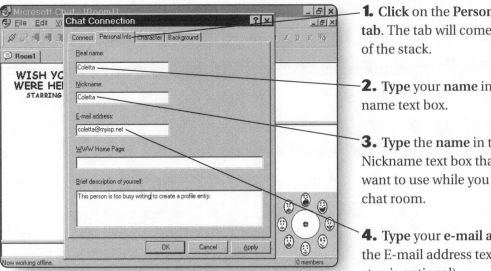

1. **Click** on the **Personal Info tab**. The tab will come to the top of the stack.

2. **Type** your **name** in the Real name text box.

3. **Type** the **name** in the Nickname text box that you want to use while you are in a chat room.

4. **Type** your **e-mail address** in the E-mail address text box (this step is optional).

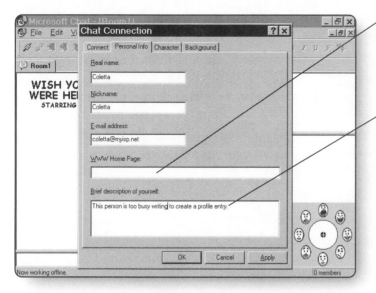

5. Type the URL of your personal Web page in the WWW Home Page text box (this step is optional).

6. Type any personal information that you want to make available to other chat room participants in the Brief description of yourself text box.

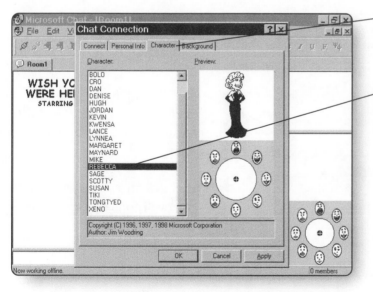

7. Click on the Character tab. The Character tab will come to the top of the stack.

8. In the Character box, click on the character that you want to have represent you in the chat session. The character will be selected.

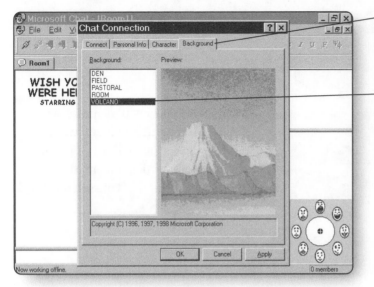

9. Click on the **Background tab**. The Background tab will come to the top of the stack.

10. Click on the **background** that you want to use for the comic strip. The background will be selected.

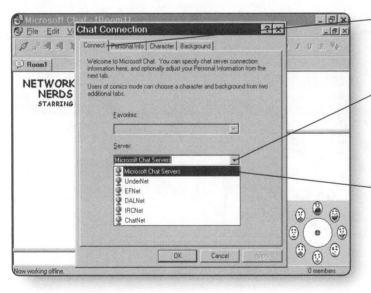

11. Click on the **Connect tab**. The Connect tab will come to the top of the stack.

12. Click on the **down-arrow** next to the Server text box. A list of available chat servers will appear.

13. Click on a **chat server**. The server will appear in the Server text box.

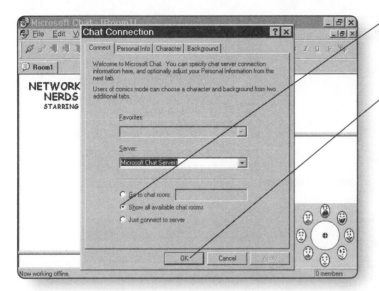

14. Click on the **Show all available chat rooms button**. The option will be selected.

15. Click on **OK**. You will be connected to the specified chat server and the Message of the Day dialog box will appear.

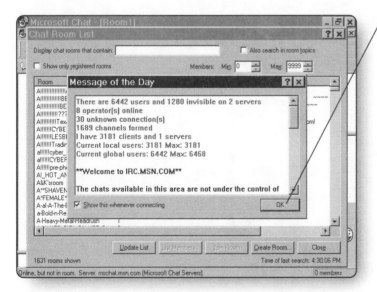

16. Click on **OK**. The Chat Room List dialog box will appear.

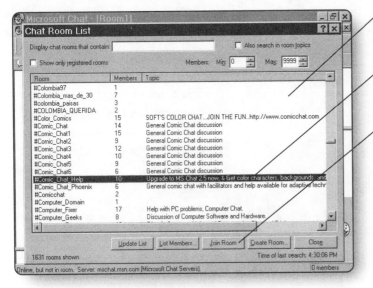

17. Browse through the **list** of chat rooms.

18. Click on a **chat room**. The chat room will be selected.

19. Click on the **Join Room** button.

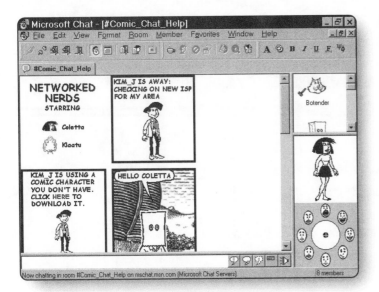

The chat room will appear in the Microsoft Chat window.

SWITCHING BETWEEN COMIC STRIP AND TEXT MODES

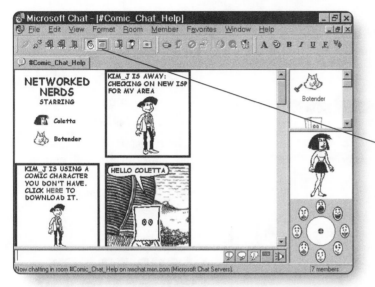

There may be times when you don't want to use the comic character features of Microsoft Chat. You can turn off the comic strip look and display the chat conversation as text only.

1. Click on the Text View button.

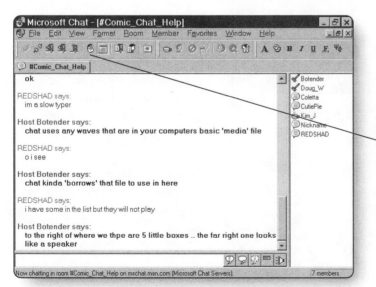

The characters in the comic strip panels will disappear and will be replaced by the names of the chat room participants.

NOTE

Click on the Comics View button to return to the comic strip view.

CHANGING THE APPEARANCE OF THE CHAT WINDOW

You can customize your chat window by altering its elements, such as changing the number of panels that appear across the window. You may want to experiment to find what works best for you.

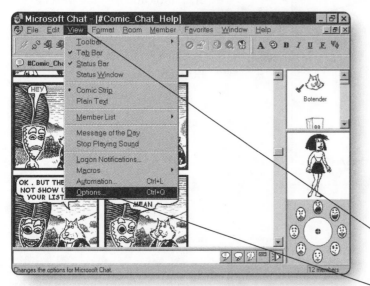

Changing How Frames Display

1. Click on **View**. The View menu will appear.

2. Click on **Options**. The Microsoft Chat Options dialog box will appear.

3. Click on the **Comics View tab**. The tab will come to the top of the stack.

4. Click the **Page layout drop-down arrow**. A list of horizontal panel display formats will appear.

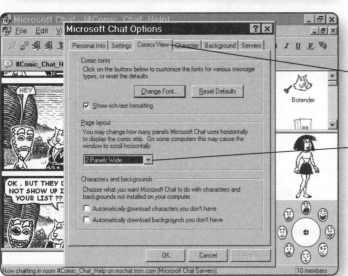

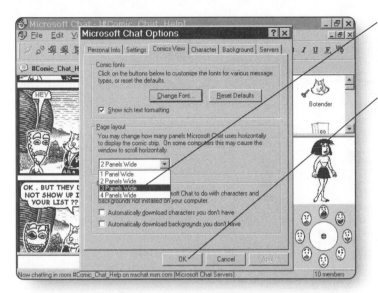

5. Click on the **number of panels** you want. The selection will appear in the list box.

6. Click on **OK**.

Your chat room view will change.

Selecting the Display Font

1. **Click** on the **Font button**. The Font dialog box will open.

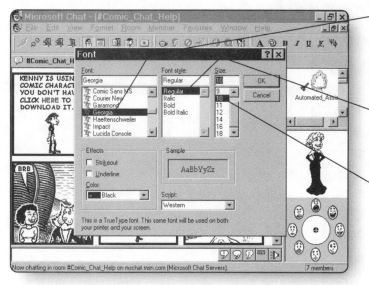

2. **Click** on the **font** in the Font list box. This font will be selected for the comic strip panels.

3. **Click** on the **font style** in the Font style list box. The font style will be selected.

4. In the Size list box, **click** on the **font size** that you want for the comic strip text. The font size will be selected.

5. **Click** on **OK**.

The new font will appear in the comic strip bubbles.

SAVING YOUR CHAT SESSIONS

When you save a chat session, it is saved in Microsoft's comic chat format. These saved files can be opened only in Microsoft Chat. Not only is the text of the chat session saved, but the comic strip panels are saved as well.

1. **Click** on **File**. The File menu will appear.

2. **Click** on **Save**. The Save As dialog box will appear.

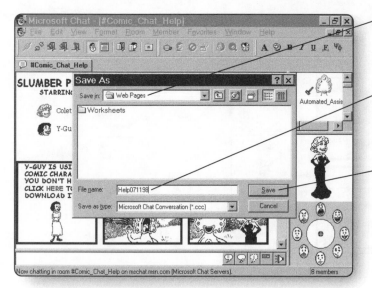

3. **Open** the **folder** in which you want to save the chat transcript. The folder will be selected.

4. **Type** a **file name** for the chat transcript in the File name text box.

5. **Click** on **Save**. The chat session will be saved and you will be able to view it at another time.

15 Participating in a Chat Group

Now that you know how to create a chat room character, you are ready to enter your first chat room. Participating in chat room discussions has always been a popular activity among Internet users. It is a great way to meet people with similar interests and discuss almost anything. This chapter provides an introduction to chat rooms and leads you through the business of joining a discussion group. In this chapter, you'll learn how to:

✦ Locate and move between chat rooms

✦ Participate in chat room discussions

✦ Contact other chat participants

✦ Use Web addresses in chat discussions

✦ Acquire additional chat characters

FINDING A CHAT ROOM

The Internet offers thousands of chat rooms, covering virtually every subject. The vast assortment can sometimes seem overwhelming. Luckily, there is a way to sort through the lists of chat rooms to find ones you will truly enjoy.

Joining a New Chat Room

Getting started in a chat room is as easy as deciding which subject you'd most like to discuss.

1. **Click** on the **Chat Room List button**. The Chat Room List dialog box will open.

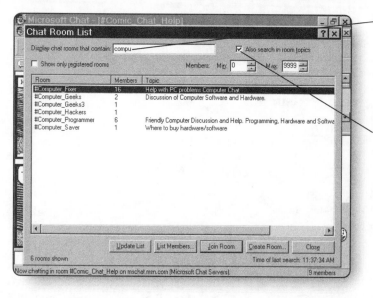

2. In the Display chat rooms that contain text box, **type a word** that describes the type of chat room discussion you are seeking.

3. **Click** on **Also search in room topics** to look for your search word within the chat room descriptions. A check mark will appear in the box.

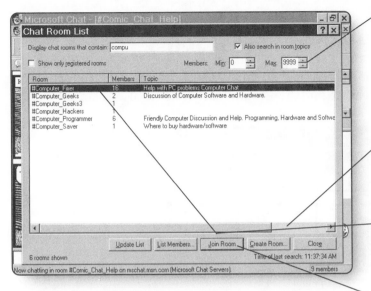

4. Click repeatedly on the **up** and **down arrows** next to the Min and Max boxes to set the minimum and maximum number of people with whom you want to share the chat room.

5. Use the **scroll bar** to look through the list of chat rooms that meet your criteria.

6. Click on the **room** that you want to visit. The chat room will be selected.

7. Click on **Join Room**.

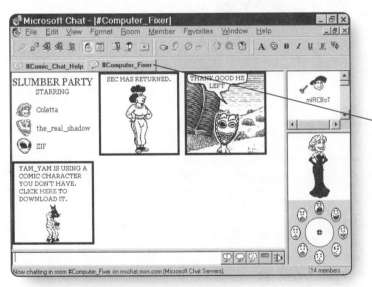

The selected chat discussion will appear in the chat window and you can join the discussion.

TIP

You can move from room to room by clicking on a room's tab.

Accessing Your Favorite Chat Rooms

You may enjoy chatting in a few different rooms. You can make it easy to find those rooms each time you use Microsoft Chat.

1. Click on **Favorites**. The Favorites menu will appear.

2. Click on **Add to Favorites**. A confirmation dialog box will appear.

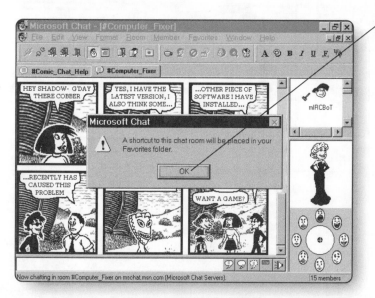

3. Click on **OK**. A shortcut to the room will be added to your list of favorites. You will be able to access the rooms that you visit frequently from the Favorites menu.

4. **Click** on **Favorites**. The Favorites menu will appear.

5. **Click** on a **room**. The room will appear in the chat window.

TIP

You can find your chat room favorites list on any Favorites menu (such as in the browser and on the Windows Start menu).

PARTICIPATING IN THE CHAT DISCUSSION

Now that you've spent some time finding good places to chat (maybe lurking around some) and familiarized yourself with how Microsoft Chat works, it's time to start making chat friends and joining the conversations.

Asking Questions First

After you read some of the comments in the discussion, you may want to take part. Help is available to members of some moderated chat rooms, and here's how to find it.

1. **Read** the **chat panels** to see whether any type of automated help is available.

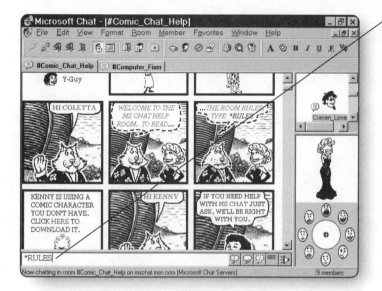

2. Type the **commands** specified in the panels for help and press the Enter key. The request will display.

3. Read the chat room **rules** and follow them. Failure to follow the rules will get you kicked out of a room.

Speaking Up

Someone has just said something on which you wish to comment. While text is the major element in a chat discussion, use special elements to give expression to your text.

1. **Click** on the **character** to which you want to respond. The character will be selected.

2. **Press and hold** the **mouse button** on the black dot and **drag** it around the circle to set the facial expression for your character. The character's expression will appear in the preview pane.

3. **Release** the **mouse button** on the desired expression. The expression will be selected.

4. **Type** your **message** in the text box.

5. **Click** on the **Talk button**.

Your message will appear in a chat panel.

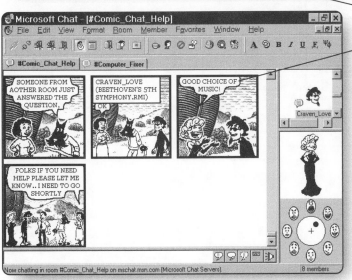

6. Type a **thought** in the text box at the bottom of the screen.

7. Click on the **Think button**.

Your thought will appear in a thought bubble.

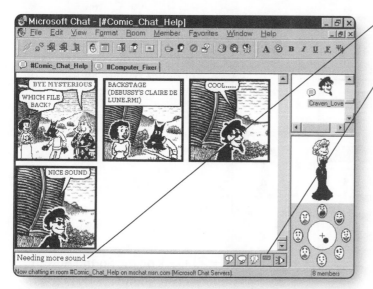

8. Type an **action** in the text box at the bottom of the screen.

9. Click on the **Action** button.

Your name will appear before the action in an action box.

Playing Sounds

You can also enhance the chat experience with the addition of sound. You can play sounds to accompany what your character is saying.

1. **Select** an **expression** for your character (see the previous section, "Speaking Up," if you don't remember how to do this).

2. **Click** on the **Sound button**. The Play Sound dialog box will open.

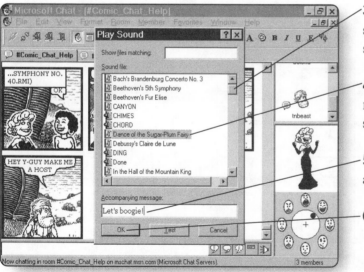

3. **Drag** the mouse along the **scroll bar** until you see the sound that you want to play.

4. **Click** on the **sound**. The name of the sound will be selected.

5. **Type** a **message** to accompany the sound.

6. **Click** on **OK**.

The message will appear and the sound will play.

Whispering in a Chat Room

If you want to send a private message to an individual or a group, try whispering. When you whisper to selected individuals, only you and they will see the whispered message. It will not appear in the chat windows of other chat room members.

1. Select a facial expression for your character.

2. Click on the character to whom you want to send a private message.

3. Type the message.

4. Click on the Whisper button.

Only you and the person to whom you sent the whispered message will see the message.

TIP

To whisper to a group, click on the first person, press and hold the Ctrl key, and click on the other people to whom you want to whisper.

CONNECTING WITH OTHERS

Your contact with fellow chatters isn't limited to being in a chat room with them. You may want to contact someone by e-mail and have a private conversation. Or, you may want to see if they're lurking around the same chat server you are, so that you can ask them to join you in a chat conversation.

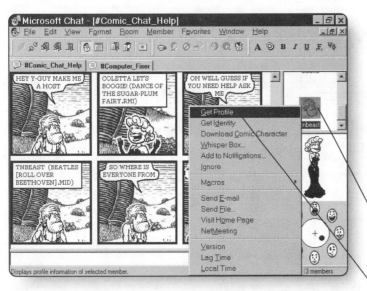

Getting Personal Information

Some people make personal information about themselves available to anyone who wants to look for it. Here's a sample of what you can find out about a person.

1. **Right-click** on the **person** for whom you want more information. A menu will appear.

2. **Click** on **Get Profile**.

The person's profile will appear in a comic strip panel along with his or her comic character.

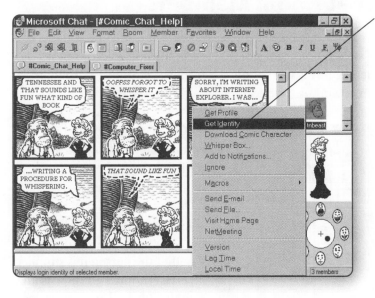

3. Click on Get Identity.

The person's e-mail address will appear in a comic strip panel along with his or her comic character.

Sending E-mail to Chat Room Members

If you want to correspond privately with someone you meet in a chat room, you can try to send the person an e-mail message. This works only if they have chosen to make their e-mail address public.

1. **Click** on the **member** to whom you want to send an e-mail message. The member's icon will be selected.

2. **Click** on the **E-mail button**. Microsoft Chat will determine whether the person has supplied an e-mail address. If there is an e-mail address, a new message window will open with your default e-mail program (for example, Outlook Express).

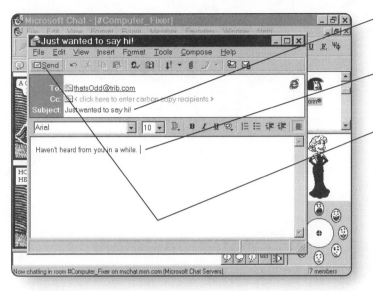

3. Type a **subject** for your message in the Subject area.

4. Type your **message** in the message area.

5. Click on the **Send button**. Your e-mail message will be sent to the recipient.

Inviting Others to Join a Chat

As you go chatting around, you will meet people with whom you enjoy talking. At times you may be in a chat room, having a great conversation, and want to invite someone else to participate. Here's how you can find that person and invite them to join a chat discussion.

1. Click on the **User List button**. The User List dialog box will open.

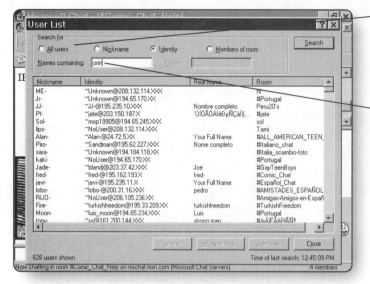

2. **Click** on the **option button** that corresponds to the type of search you want to perform. The option will be selected.

3. **Type** the **name or nickname** of the person you are seeking in the Names containing text box.

4. **Click** on **Search**. A list of names will appear.

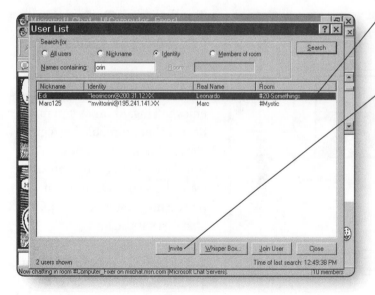

5. **Click** on the **name** of the person matching your search. The name will be selected.

6. **Click** on **Invite**. A message will be sent to that person asking whether he or she wants to join the discussion in your chat room, and a confirmation dialog box will appear.

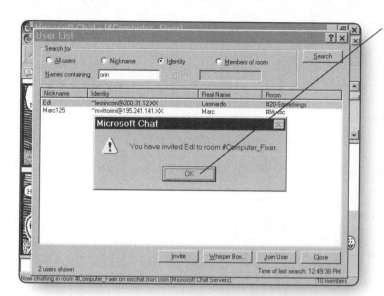

7. Click on OK.

TIP

If you want to join a chat room in which someone else is chatting, click on Join User.

USING URL ADDRESSES DURING A CHAT SESSION

Web addresses can be displayed to make it easy for chat members to access Web pages during a chat session.

Displaying a URL Address

1. Select an **expression** for your character (see "Speaking Up" in this chapter if you don't remember how to do this).

2. Type a **URL address** in the text box at the bottom of the screen.

3. Press the **Enter key**.

The URL address will appear in blue text in a panel.

Accessing Web Pages

You may access a Web page directly from its URL address shown in the chat panel.

1. Double-click on the URL address.

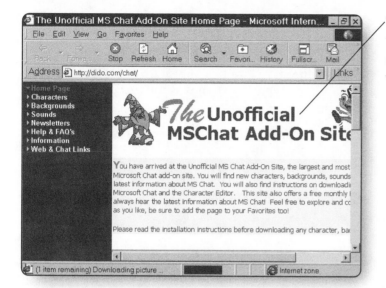

The Web page associated with the URL address will download and open in an Internet Explorer window.

GETTING MORE CHAT CHARACTERS

1. Locate a comic strip panel that tells you a person is using a character that you don't have installed on your computer.

2. Click on the blue HERE text within the panel. The character file will be downloaded to your computer.

NOTE

This character file will be available for you to use when you visit chat rooms. To use the new character, open the View menu and select Options. Click on the Character tab in the Options dialog box. You'll see the recently downloaded character in the list.

MORE CHARACTERS AND SOUNDS

Here are some places where you can find additional characters to suit your personality and sounds that other chat participants may use that you don't yet have in your repertoire.

The Unofficial Microsoft Chat Add-On Site at **www.dido.com/chat/.**

The Official Microsoft Chat Site at **www.microsoft.com/ie/chat/.**

16 Getting Ready for Video Conferencing

Feeling comfortable with your environment is essential to good communication. Being in a familiar environment and feeling that you are in control will always make things work much more smoothly. Taking the time now to learn your way around the NetMeeting screen and become familiar with the screen elements and options will enable you to participate in upcoming meetings with ease. In this chapter, you'll learn how to:

✦ Set up NetMeeting

✦ Block incoming calls during a conference

✦ Find NetMeeting servers

✦ Create SpeedDial entries

✦ Adjust the volume of your NetMeeting sessions

SETTING UP NETMEETING FOR THE FIRST TIME

When you first start NetMeeting, a wizard will help you set up your system for future conferences. Once you've run through the following steps, you can start video-conferencing with family and friends.

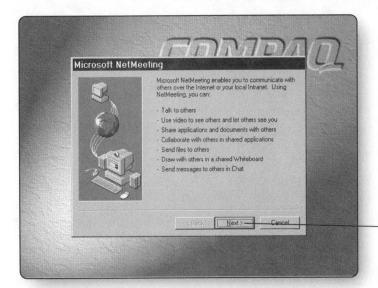

1. Click on **Next**. The directory server screen will appear.

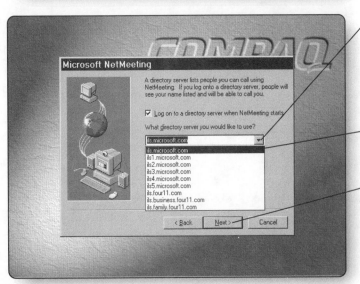

2. Click on the **down arrow** next to the What directory server would you like to use? list box. A list of available servers will appear.

3. Click on a **server**. The server will be selected.

4. Click on **Next**. The personal information screen will appear.

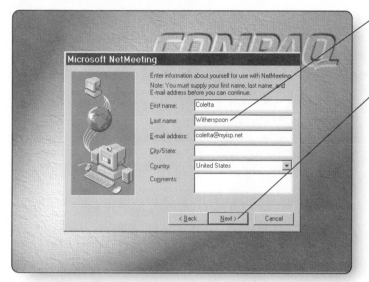

5. Type only the **information** about yourself that you want to make public.

6. Click on **Next**. The category screen will appear.

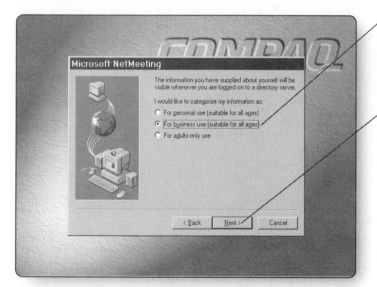

7. Click on the **option button** that corresponds to the category you want to use. The option will be selected.

8. Click on **Next**. The modem screen will appear.

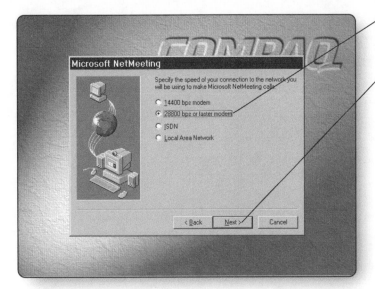

9. **Click** on your **modem speed**. The option will be selected.

10. **Click** on Next. The Audio Tuning screen will appear.

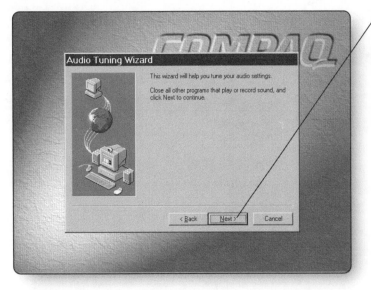

11. **Click** on Next. The wave device screen will appear.

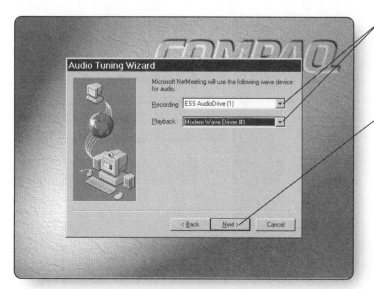

12. **Select** your **recording and playback wave devices**. The wave devices will show in the list boxes.

13. **Click** on **Next**. The volume test screen will appear.

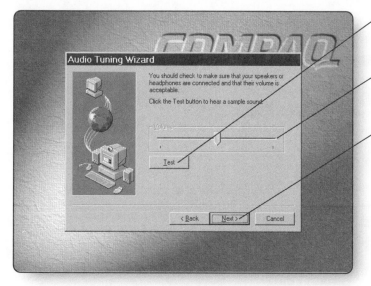

14. **Click** on the **Test button**. A sound will play.

15. **Adjust** the volume **slider** and retest if needed.

16. **Click** on **Next**. The microphone volume screen will appear.

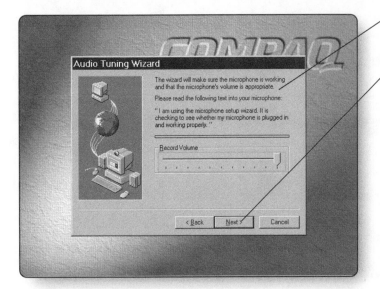

17. **Read** the **text** into your computer's microphone.

18. **Click** on **Next**. The last screen will appear.

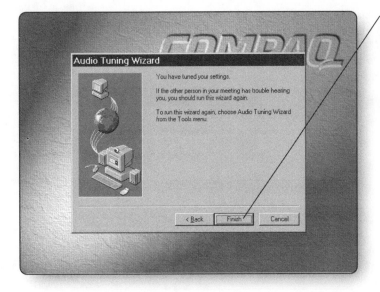

19. **Click** on **Finish**. NetMeeting will start.

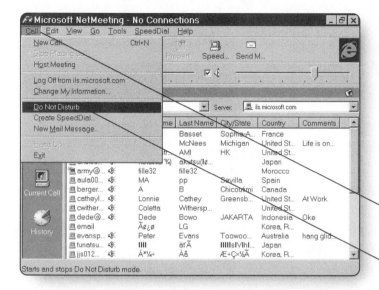

BLOCKING INCOMING CALLS

NetMeeting can be set to reject incoming calls if you don't want to be disturbed during an online conference.

1. **Click** on **Call**. The Call menu will appear.

2. **Click** on **Do Not Disturb**. A dialog box will open.

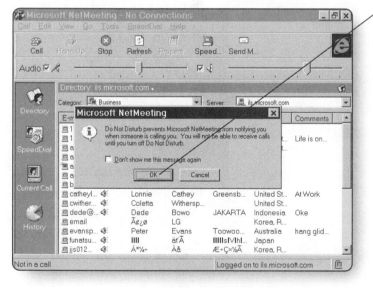

3. **Click** on **OK**. NetMeeting will not answer incoming calls.

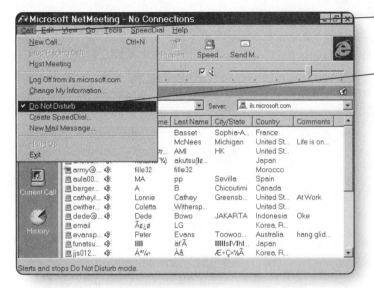

4. **Click** on **Call**. The Call menu will open.

5. **Click** on **Do Not Disturb**. The check mark will disappear and NetMeeting will go back to answering incoming calls.

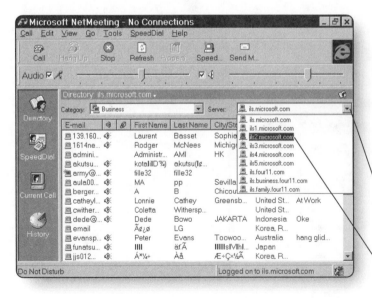

SEARCHING FOR ILS LISTINGS

You may want to find other servers that have NetMeeting participants.

1. **Click** on the **down arrow** next to the Server list box. A list of NetMeeting servers will appear.

2. **Click** on a **server**.

The server will appear in the list box, and the people logged into that server will be listed below it.

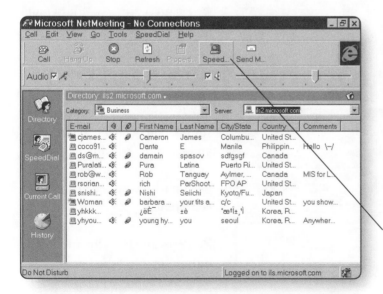

CREATING SPEEDDIAL ENTRIES

If you conference with certain people on a regular basis, simplify the connection by storing their NetMeeting address in the SpeedDial list.

1. **Click** on the **Add SpeedDial button**. The Add SpeedDial dialog box will open.

2. In the Address text box, **type** the **IP Address** or **e-mail address** of the person that you wish to add to the SpeedDial list.

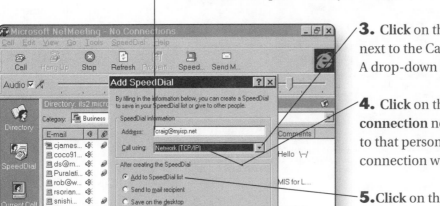

3. **Click** on the **down arrow** next to the Call using list box. A drop-down list will appear.

4. **Click** on the type of **network connection** needed to connect to that person. The network connection will be selected.

5. Click on the **Add to SpeedDial list option** to add this entry to your SpeedDial list. The option will be selected.

6. **Click** on **OK**. A new entry will be created in the SpeedDial list.

ADJUSTING THE VOLUME

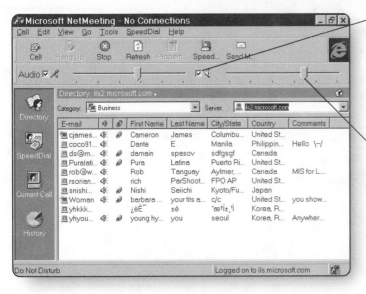

1. **Click** in the box next to the **sound icon**. A check mark will appear in the box and you will be able to hear the voice of the person with whom you are conferencing.

2. **Press and hold** the **mouse button** on the slider bar and **drag** it to adjust your speaker volume.

3. **Release** the **mouse button** when you reach the desired volume. The volume level will be selected.

17 Participating in NetMeeting Conferences

Videoconferences are a great way to keep in touch with family, friends, and business associates. When e-mail just won't do, try NetMeeting for some real-time, true voice conversations, complete with video and spoken words. With NetMeeting, you can place a call to someone, and not only speak with them, but also share video (if you are both video-enabled), discuss ideas with a whiteboard, and send files back and forth. You'll have lots of fun keeping in contact with everyone. In this chapter, you'll learn how to:

✦ Connect to people through a NetMeeting server

✦ Use the chat tool when you don't want to use your voice

✦ Share ideas and images with an online Whiteboard

CONNECTING TO OTHERS

There are many ways to connect with people using NetMeeting. On NetMeeting servers you can find old acquaintances and meet new friends, either through an Internet search or by dialing them directly. For people that you call frequently, you'll want to keep track of them using SpeedDial.

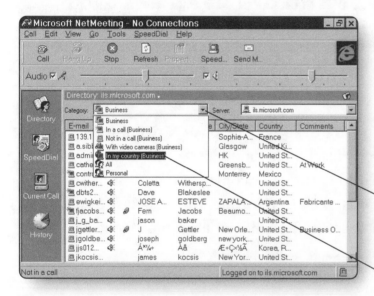

Finding a NetMeeting Server

The following steps will lead you through the process of finding a NetMeeting server and making your first NetMeeting call.

1. Click on the **down arrow** next to the Category list box. A list of categories will appear.

2. Click on the **category** that includes the type of people with whom you want to conference. The category will show in the Category list box, and the list of people logged onto the server will be updated.

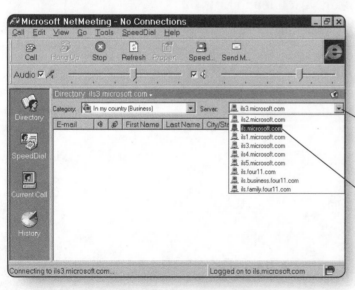

3. Click on the **down arrow** next to the Server list box for a list of available conference servers.

4. Click on the **conference server** that you want to access. The server will appear in the Server list box, and the directory list for the server will download.

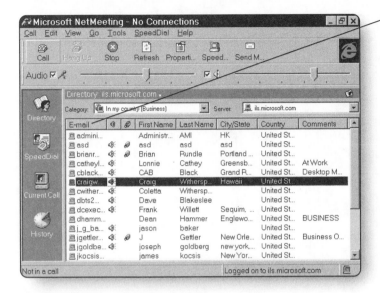

5. Click on the **E-mail column**. The directory list will sort alphabetically by e-mail address.

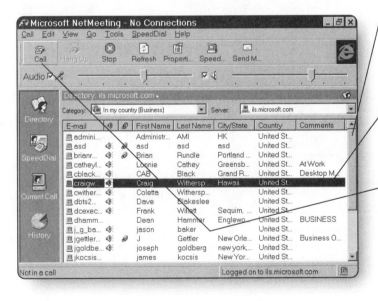

6. Scroll through the **directory listing** until you find the person with whom you want to conference.

7. Click on the **listing** for that person. The listing will be highlighted.

8. Click on the **Call button**. The New Call dialog box will open.

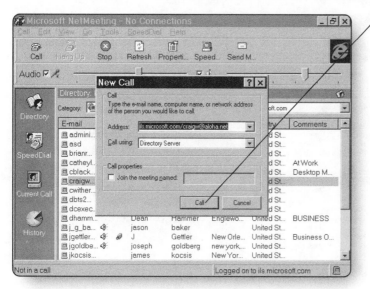

9. Click on **Call**. NetMeeting will attempt to connect with the other person.

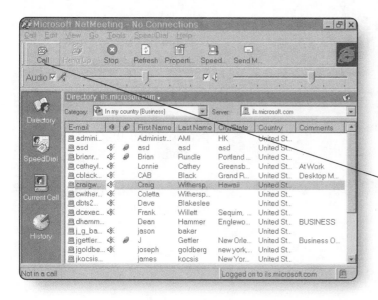

Calling Directly on the Internet

If you know the IP address of the person with whom you wish to conference, you can connect directly over the Internet.

1. Click on the **Call button**. The New Call dialog box will open.

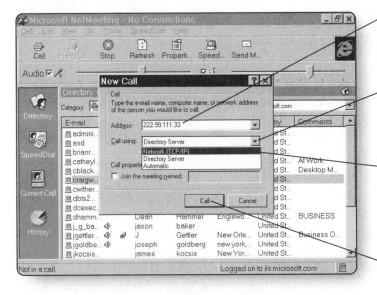

2. In the Address box, **type** the **IP Address** of the person with whom you want to conference.

3. Click on the **down arrow** next to the Call using list box for a list of contact methods.

4. Click on **Network (TCP/IP)** from the drop-down list. Network (TCP/IP) will be selected.

5. Click on **Call**. NetMeeting will attempt to call the person with whom you want to conference.

Using SpeedDial

SpeedDial will help you keep track of people you want to call and will also allow you to connect to them. To add new entries to your SpeedDial, see "Creating SpeedDial Entries," in Chapter 16.

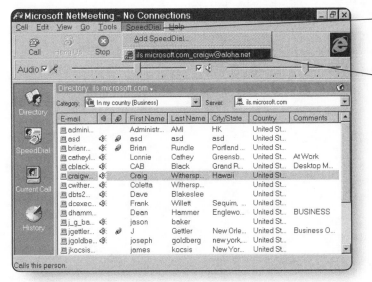

1. Click on **SpeedDial**. The SpeedDial menu will appear.

2. Click on the **SpeedDial entry** for the person you want to call. NetMeeting will attempt to connect to the person you are trying to call.

USING CHAT TO HAVE A PRIVATE CONVERSATION

If you are having problems with the audio feature of NetMeeting, you can always use the Chat tool. You can also use the Chat feature if you want to say something to one person in your conference and not to the others. The Chat tool in NetMeeting works much the same way as Microsoft Chat (except it does not use the comic characters). You type what you want to say, press a button, and your words appear in the chat window.

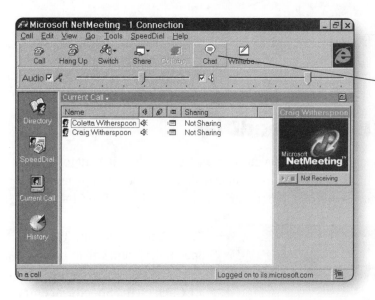

Opening the Chat Window

1. Click on the **Chat button** to access the Chat tool. The Chat tool will also appear for the other people in the conference.

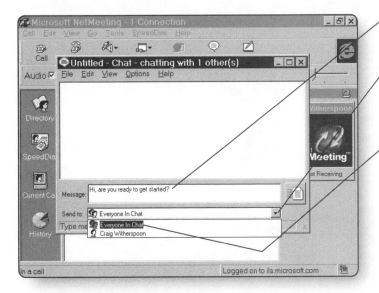

2. Type your **message** in the Message text box.

3. Click on the **down arrow** next to the Send to list box. A drop-down list will appear.

4. Click on the **people** with whom you want to share the message. Your selection will be highlighted.

5. Click on the **Post button**.

Your message will be visible in the chat area.

Any messages posted by others in your conference will also appear.

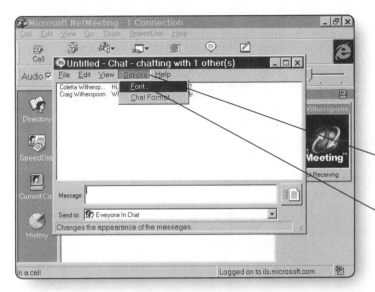

Changing the Chat Format

You can easily change the Chat options to suit your needs or wishes.

1. **Click** on **Options**. The Options menu will appear.

2. **Click** on **Font**. The Font dialog box will open.

3. In the Font box, **click** on the **font** that you want to use to display text in the Chat tool window. The font will be selected.

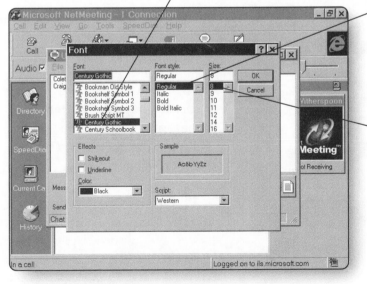

4. In the Font style box, **click** on the **font style** that you want to use for text in the Chat tool window. The font style will be selected.

5. In the Size box, **click** on the **font size** that you want to use to display the text in the Chat tool window. The size will be selected.

6. **Click** on **OK**. The font within the Chat tool window will change.

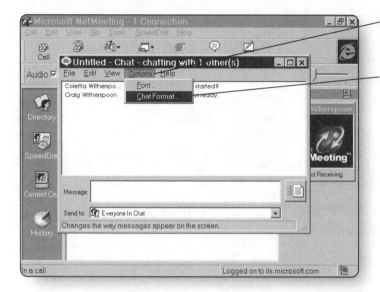

7. Click on **Options** for the Options menu.

8. Click on **Chat Format**. The Chat Format dialog box will open.

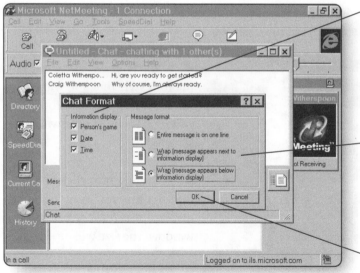

9. Click on those **items** in the Information display area that you want to display in the Chat tool window. A check mark will appear in the box next to each item you select.

10. In the Message format area, click on the **option button** for the format in which you want to display Chat messages. The option will be selected.

11. Click on OK.

The format of the Chat tool window will change.

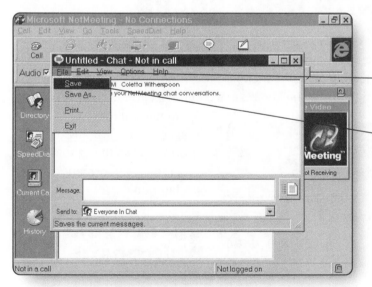

Saving the Chat Conversation

1. **Click** on **File**. The File menu will appear.

2. **Click** on **Save**. The Save As dialog box will open.

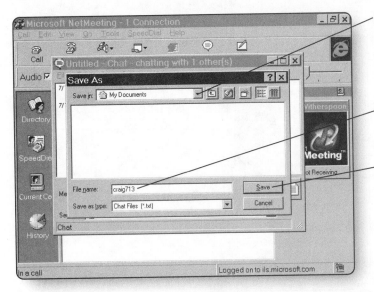

3. In the Save in box, **select** the **folder** where you want to save your Chat conversation. The folder will be selected.

4. **Type** a **name** for the Chat file in the File name text box.

5. **Click** on **Save**. The chat file will be stored on your computer.

MAKING YOUR POINT WITH WHITEBOARD

Take advantage of the power of the Whiteboard tool in your NetMeeting sessions. You can share ideas and keep track of a meeting on the Whiteboard tool in the same way that you might use a chalkboard in a conference room. NetMeeting's Whiteboard allows you to add images to your text, highlight information so that it stands out, and save information to use at a later time.

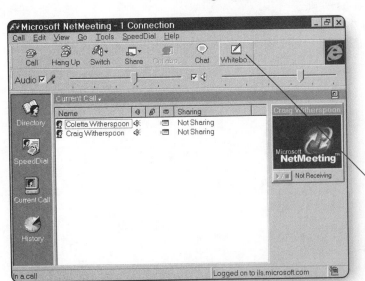

Opening the Whiteboard

1. **Click** on the **Whiteboard** button.

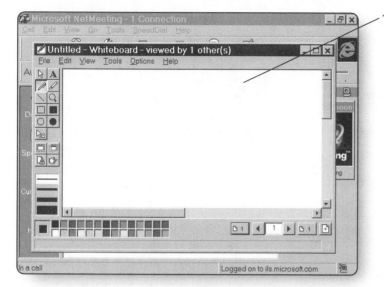

The Whiteboard will open.

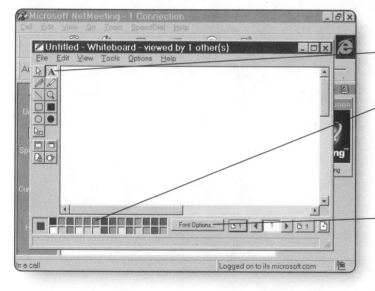

Adding Text

1. **Click** on the **Text Tool button**. The Text Tool will be selected.

2. **Click** on the **color** that you want to use for the text. The color will appear in the selected color box to the left of the color palette.

3. **Click** on **Font Options**. The Font dialog box will open.

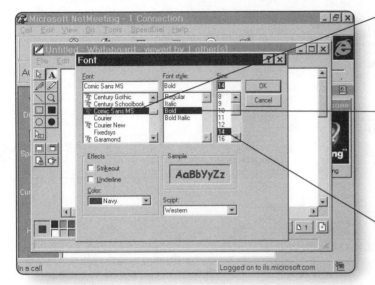

4. In the Font box, **click** on the **font** that you want to use for the text in the Chat tool window. The font will be selected.

5. In the Font style box, **click** on the **font style** that you want to use to display the text in the Chat tool window. The font style will be selected.

6. In the Size box, **click** on the **font size** that you want to use to display the text in the Chat tool window. The size will be selected.

7. Click on **OK**. The Whiteboard tool will return.

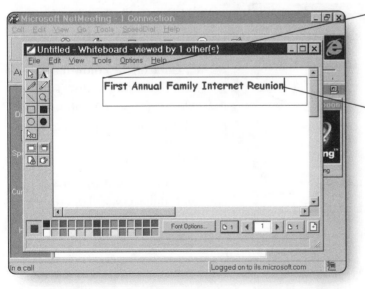

8. Click on the **location** where you want to place your text. A cursor will appear, outlined by a black box.

9. Type your **text**. The text will display on the Whiteboard and all of the conference participants will be able to see it.

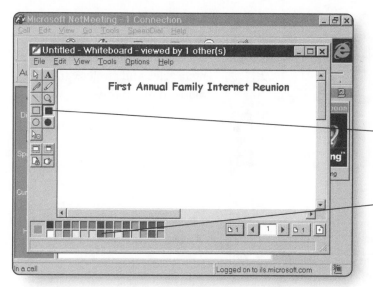

Adding Shapes

You can add shapes to your Whiteboard presentation by selecting them from the toolbar.

1. **Click** on the **Filled Rectangle tool button**. The Filled Rectangle tool will be selected.

2. **Click** on the **color** that you want the rectangle to be. The color will appear in the selected color box.

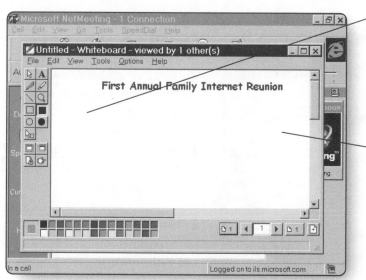

3. **Press and hold** the **mouse button** on the location where you want to start the rectangle and **drag** the mouse pointer to the location where you want to end the rectangle.

4. **Release** the **mouse button**.

A filled rectangle will appear on the Whiteboard. Straight lines, filled circles, and transparent rectangles and circles can be made in much the same way.

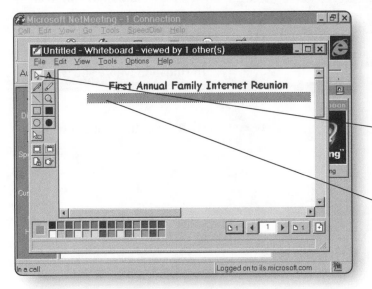

Moving Objects

You can move things around on the Whiteboard by using the mouse.

1. **Click** on the **Selector tool button**. The mouse cursor will change to an arrow.

2. **Click** on the **object** that you want to move. A dotted border will outline the object.

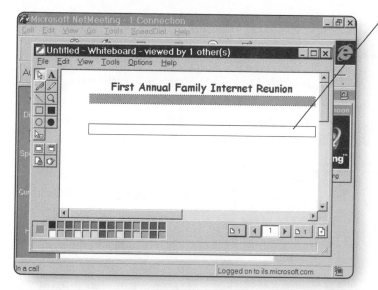

3. Press and hold the mouse button on the object while you drag the object toward the desired position.

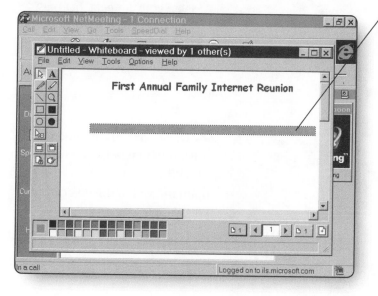

4. Release the mouse button when the object is positioned where you want it. The object will be moved to the new position.

Adding Images to the Whiteboard

Images may be added to your Whiteboard presentation by using the Whiteboard tools. Minimize the Whiteboard window and access the program containing the object that you want to display.

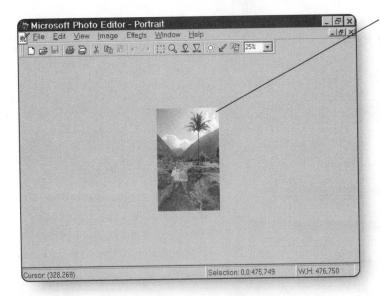

1. **Display** the **object** that you want to copy to the Whiteboard.

NOTE

You can use text or graphics from any program that you have installed on your computer. You can even copy objects that may be located on your desktop and place them on the NetMeeting whiteboard.

2. **Click** on the **Whiteboard button** to maximize the window. The Whiteboard window will open in front of the object that you want to copy.

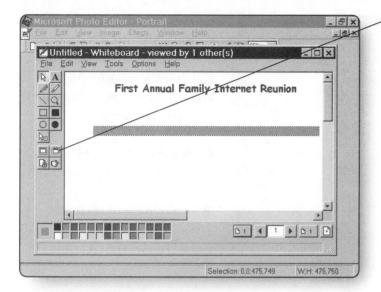

3. Click on the **Select Area tool**. The Whiteboard Select Area dialog box will open.

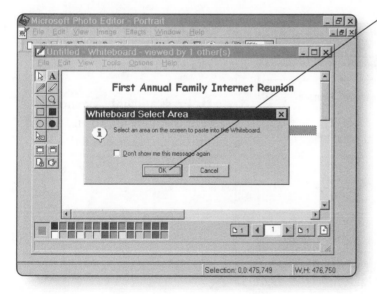

4. Click on OK. The Whiteboard will minimize itself, and the object that you want to copy will appear.

5. Press and hold the mouse button at the upper-left corner of the area that you want to copy and drag the mouse to the lower-right corner. A dotted line will surround the selected area.

6. Release the mouse button. The selection will be copied and pasted into the upper-left corner of the Whiteboard window.

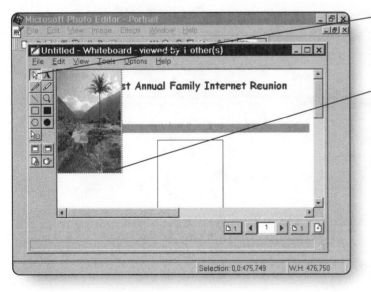

7. Click on the Selector tool button. The mouse cursor will change to an arrow.

8. Press and hold the mouse button on the object and drag the object to the desired position.

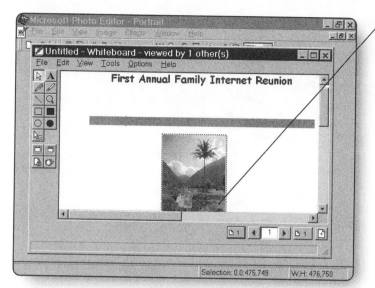

9. **Release** the **mouse button**. The object will move to the desired location.

Saving Whiteboard Contents

1. **Click** on **File**. The File menu will appear.

2. **Click** on **Save**. The Save As dialog box will open.

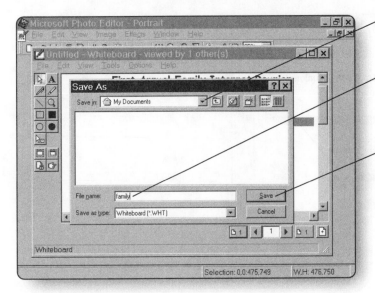

3. **Select** the **folder** where the file is to be saved.

4. **Type** a **name** for the Whiteboard file in the File name text box.

5. **Click** on **Save**. The file will be saved to the selected folder on your computer.

18 Sharing Documents During a Conference

One of the most useful aspects of a meeting or conference is the opportunity for the people involved to share information while everyone is looking at the same documents. With NetMeeting, the group can also share applications, as you will see by following along through this section. In this chapter, you'll learn how to:

✦ Share an application and make changes to a file during a conference

✦ Transfer to and receive files from other conference participants

SHARING APPLICATIONS

It is often easier to accomplish a meeting's task if everyone in the group can work on it together. For example, you can share a Word document across the Internet with someone who doesn't have Word, allowing that person to work in your Word application.

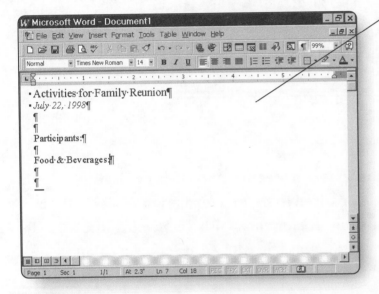

1. Open the **application** and the **document** that you want to share during the conference.

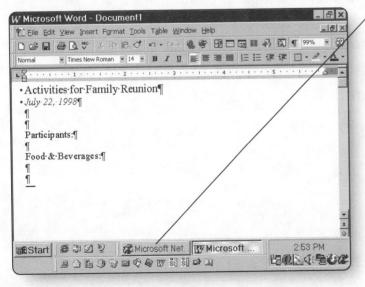

2. Click on the **NetMeeting icon** on the Windows taskbar. You will switch to the NetMeeting window.

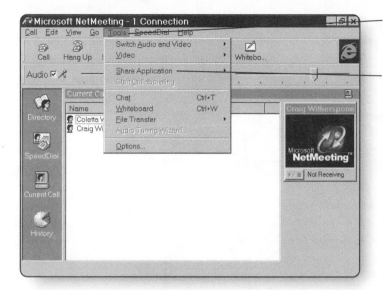

3. Click on **Tools**. The Tools menu will appear.

4. Click on **Share Application**. A cascading menu will appear.

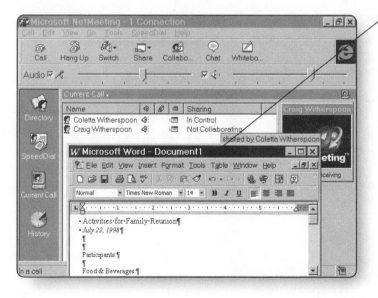

5. Click on the name of the **application and document** that you want to share. A dialog box will open.

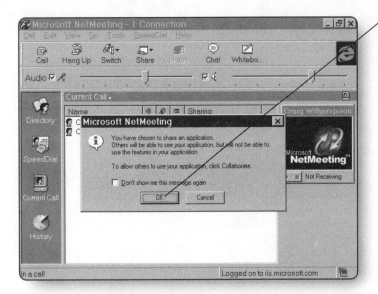

6. Click on **OK**. Everyone in the conference will be able to see the document but will not be able to make any changes to it.

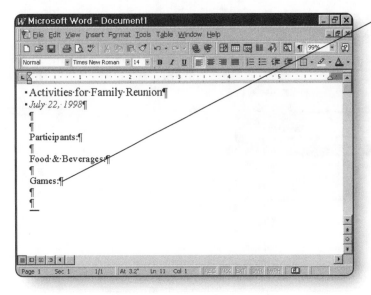

7. **Make** any **changes** to the document as needed. The changes will appear on each person's screen.

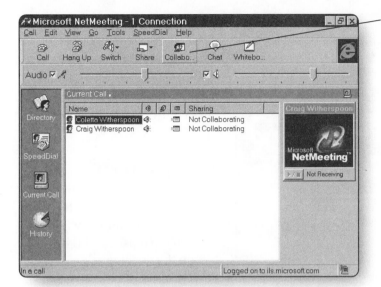

8. Click on the **Collaborate button**. A dialog box will open.

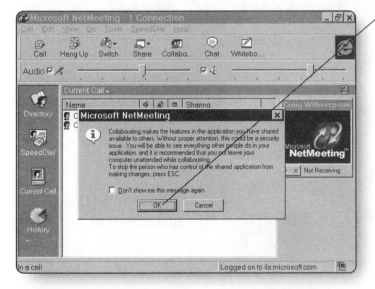

9. Click on **OK**. Everyone in the conference will be able to make changes to the document.

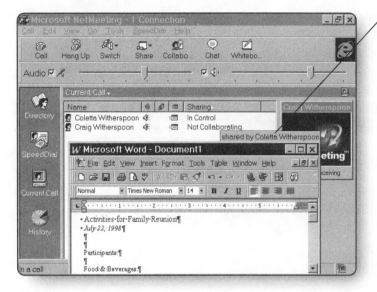

10. **Click** anywhere on your computer **screen** to take control of the document and make changes. The Current Call tab will be on top and will show who has control of the document.

NOTE

Make sure everyone in the conference clicks on the Collaborate button when you are finished working on the document.

TRANSFERRING FILES

Transferring files back and forth is perhaps the most popular Internet activity, and doing it through NetMeeting is easy.

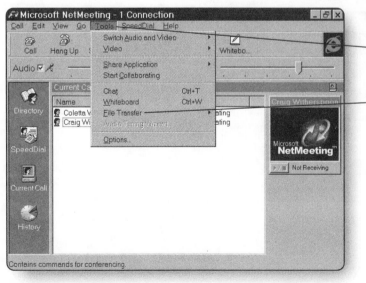

Sending a File

1. **Click** on **Tools**. The Tools menu will appear.

2. **Click** on **File Transfer**. A cascading menu will appear.

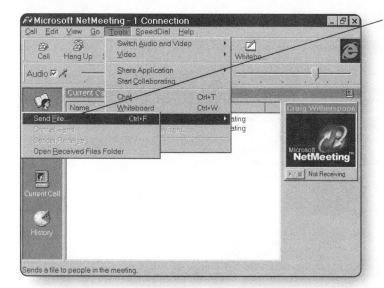

3. **Click** on **Send File**. The Select a File to Send dialog box will open.

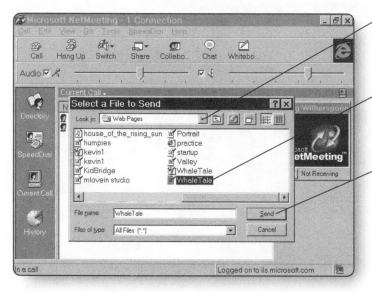

4. **Select** the **folder** in which the file you want to send is stored. The folder will be selected.

5. **Click** on the **file** that you want to send. The file name will be selected.

6. **Click** on **Send**.

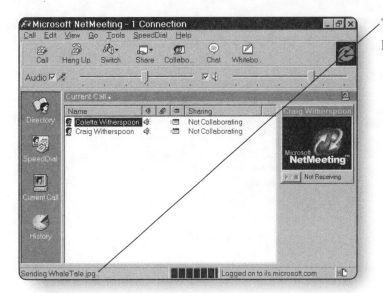

The file will be sent to the other person in your conference call.

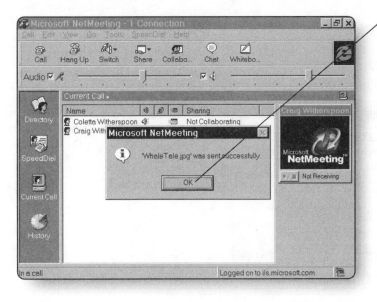

7. Click on OK.

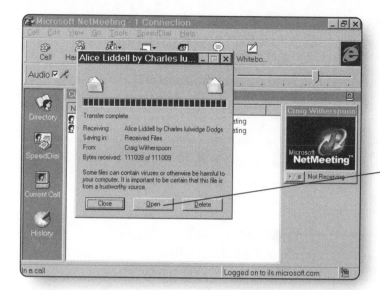

Receiving a File

Receiving a file is a simple process. It merely involves waiting because you don't want to do anything until the transfer is complete.

1. Click on **Open**. The file will open in the associated application.

2. View the **document**.

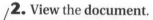

3. Click on the application's **Close button**. The file and the application will close.

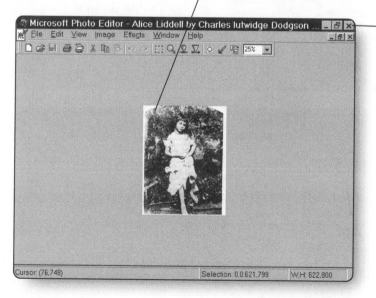

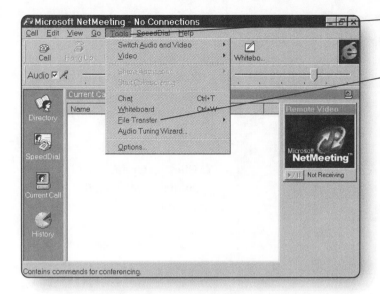

4. Click on **Tools**. The Tools menu will appear.

5. Click on **File Transfer**. A drop-down menu will appear.

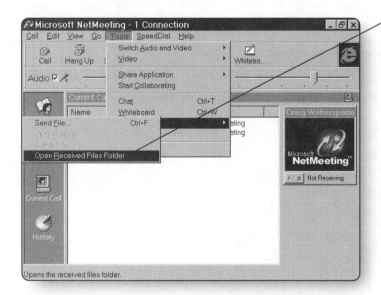

6. Click on **Open Received Files Folder**. The Received Files Folder will appear.

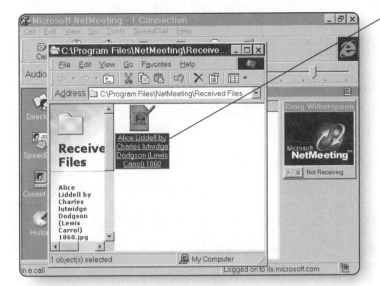

7. **Click** on the **file**. The file will open in its associated application.

PART V REVIEW QUESTIONS

1. How do you narrow down the list of chat rooms in a server so that you can more easily find the room you want to join? *See "Finding a Chat Room" in Chapter 15.*

2. What information can you obtain about the other people you are chatting with in a chat room? *See "Connecting to Others" in Chapter 15.*

3. How do you invite your friends to visit you in a particular chat room? *See "Connecting to Others" in Chapter 15.*

4. How do you tell NetMeeting not to notify you or answer incoming calls while you are in a conference call? *See "Blocking Incoming Calls" in Chapter 16.*

5. What is one way of finding an address for a person you want to contact for a conference call? *See "Searching for ILS Listings" in Chapter 16.*

6. How do you create a speed dial entry for people you call on a regular basis? *See "Creating Speed Dial Entries" in Chapter 16.*

7. How do you change the information that is recorded while you are using the NetMeeting chat tool? *See "Using Chat to Have a Private Conversation" in Chapter 17.*

8. What tools can be used to display information on the NetMeeting Whiteboard? *See "Making Your Point with Whiteboard" in Chapter 17.*

9. How does the person in control of a conference allow others to make changes to a shared document? *See "Sharing Applications" in Chapter 18.*

10. Where does NetMeeting store files that are transferred during a conference call? *See "Transferring Files" in Chapter 18.*

PART VI

Creating a Web Page with FrontPage Express

From

✉ aa
📧 M

: Microsof
ject: Welco

Micros
Ou

Welcome t

• E-mai

19 Getting Started with FrontPage Express

After you've cruised the Web for a while, you may want to create your own Web presence. If you've never created a Web page before, you might be unsure as to where to start. Well, it's easier than you think. FrontPage Express, the Web page authoring component of Internet Explorer, is a simple tool that can help you create some great looking Web pages. With a few words, a hyperlink or two, and some complementary graphics, you'll be on the Web in no time. In this chapter, you'll learn how to:

✦ Get a quick start on your Web page with wizards

✦ Add, edit, and format Web page text

✦ Save your Web page

✦ Work with FrontPage Express toolbars

GETTING STARTED WITH WIZARDS

When you first start FrontPage Express, it will open with a blank page. You could just begin working with this blank page, but there is an easier way. FrontPage Express provides a number of wizards for a quick and easy start to building a Web page. You can then fix up your Web page to include graphics, sounds, animation, and anything else that will give your Web page class.

> **NOTE**
>
> See Chapter 1, "Starting and Exiting Programs," if you need help starting the program. If FrontPage Express isn't installed on your computer, see the appendix for help getting and installing the program.

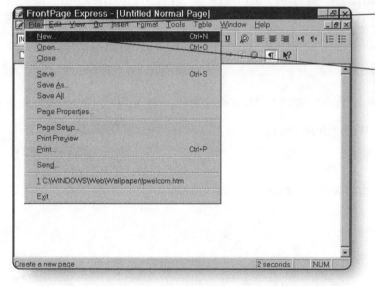

1. **Click** on **File**. The File menu will appear.

2. **Click** on **New**. The New Page dialog box will open.

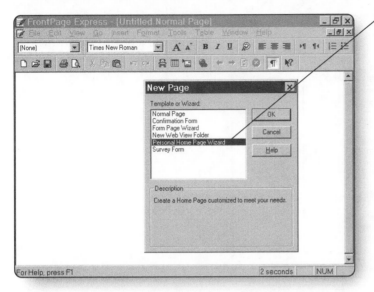

3. In the Template or Wizard box, **click** on the **wizard** that you want to use for help in building your Web page. The wizard will be selected.

NOTE

When you click on a wizard, a message in the Description area will tell you what the wizard will create.

4. **Click** on **OK**. The wizard will start.

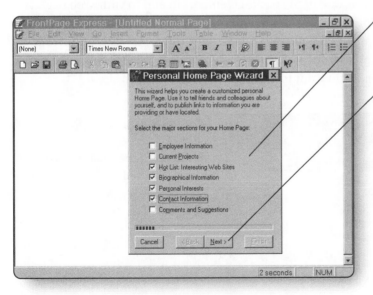

5. **Read** through each **page** of the wizard and follow the instructions.

6. As you complete each page of the wizard's questions, **click** on **Next** for the next page of the wizard. Continue until you come to the last page of the wizard.

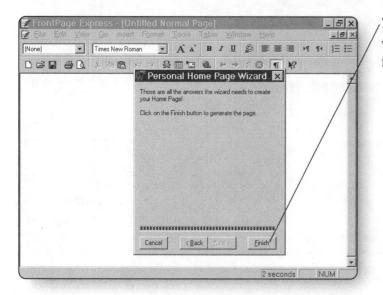

7. Click on **Finish**. The wizard will create a beginning format for your Web page.

WRITING WEB PAGE TEXT

Text is one of the easiest elements to add to your Web page. It is also the first element that you should place on the page. The words that you place on the page will set the theme for your Web site. Before you start placing text, put some thought into what you want to accomplish with your Web site.

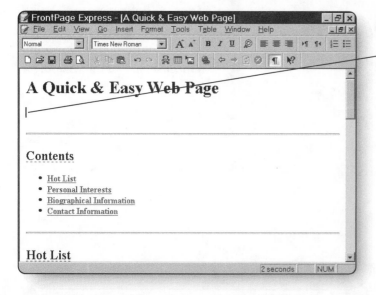

Adding Text

1. Click on the **location** where you want to place the text. The insertion bar will appear on the page.

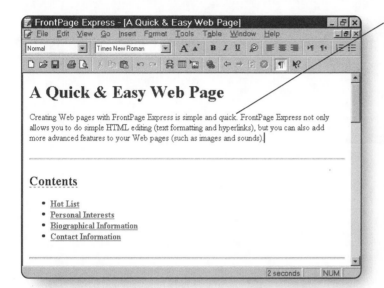

2. **Type** some **text**. The text will appear on the page.

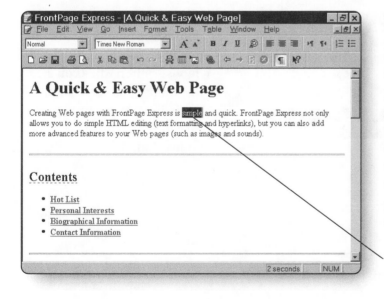

Editing Text

Before you can make any changes to the text on your Web page, you will need to select the text. Text that is selected appears as white letters on a dark background. You can only select one sequential block of text at a time, not bits of text in different places. The following shows different selection techniques:

◆ Select one word by clicking twice on the word.

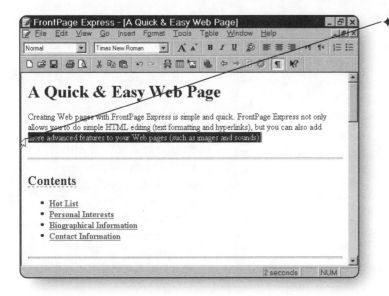

◆ Select a line by placing the mouse pointer on the left margin and clicking once next to the line.

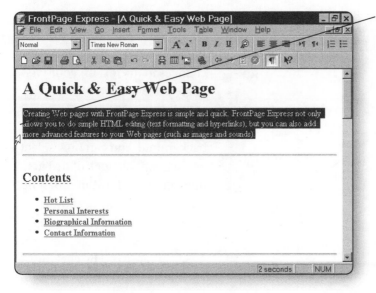

◆ Select several lines by placing the mouse pointer on the left margin. Press and hold the mouse button while you drag the mouse pointer next to each line that you want to select. Then release the mouse button.

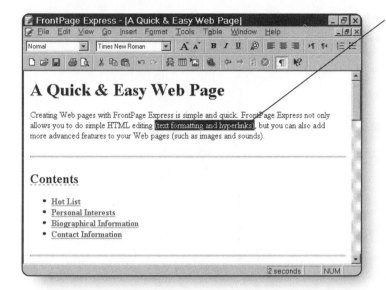

✦ Select a block of text by clicking at the beginning of the text. Press and hold the mouse button while you drag the pointer across the text until you get to the end of your selection. Then release the mouse button.

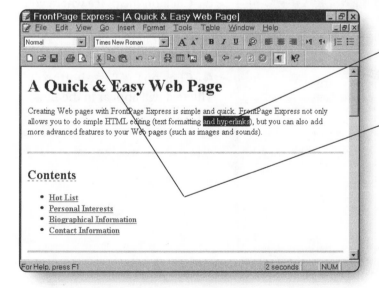

Deleting Text

1. **Select** the **text** you want to delete. The text will be highlighted.

2. **Click** on the **Cut button**. The text will disappear.

TIP

If you make a mistake and delete the wrong text or too much text, click on Edit on the menu bar. Then choose Undo Cut.

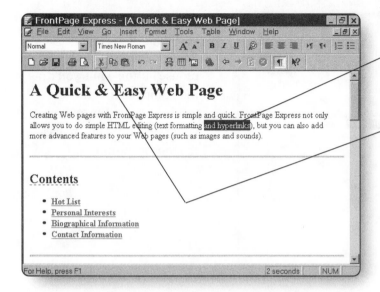

Moving Text

1. **Select** the **text** you want to move. The text will be highlighted.

2. **Click** on the **Cut button.** The text will disappear and be stored in the Windows clipboard.

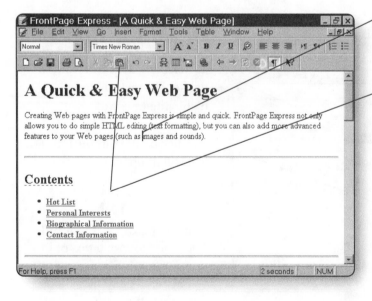

3. **Click** on the **place** where you want the text moved. The insertion bar will appear.

4. **Click** on the **Paste button.** The text will appear in the new position.

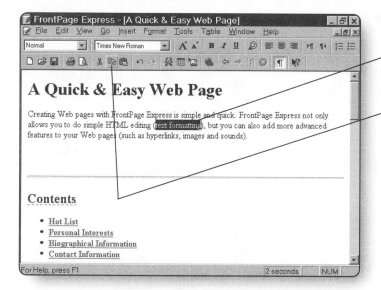

Copying Text

1. **Select** the **text** to be copied. The text will be highlighted.

2. **Click** on the **Copy button**. The text will be stored in the Windows clipboard.

3. **Click** on the **place** where you want to put a copy of the text. The insertion bar will appear.

4. **Click** on the **Paste button**. The text will be copied to the new position.

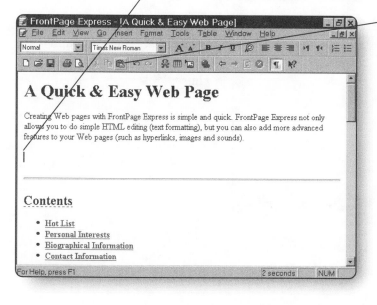

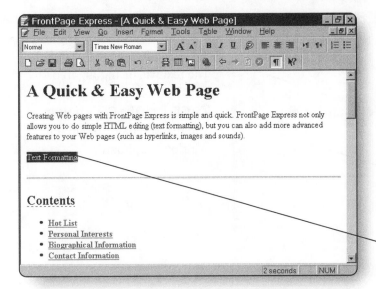

Formatting Text

Use the Format toolbar to make your text stand out. You can change the size and shape of text characters. You can turn paragraphs into bulleted or numbered lists. You can also change the alignment of paragraphs to make your words look even better.

1. Select the **text** that you want to format. The text will be highlighted.

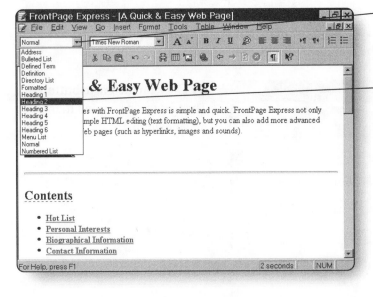

2. Click the **down-arrow** in the Change Style field. A drop-down list of style options will appear.

3. Click on a **style** that you want to use. The paragraph will be modified in the style that you chose.

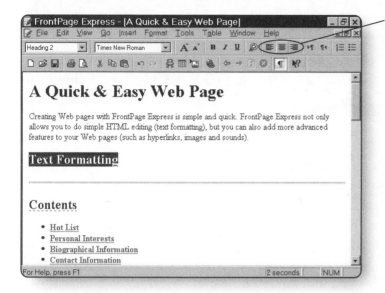

4. Click on the **Left, Center,** or **Right Alignment buttons**. The position of the text on the page will change.

SAVING WEB PAGES

The importance of saving your work can't be stressed enough. Computers are subject to a number of factors that can cause them to crash. Crashes may be caused by something as simple as an electrical surge or outage, or by something more complex, such as a hardware problem. To protect yourself from lost work, save your work every few minutes.

1. Click on the **Save button**. The Save As dialog box will open.

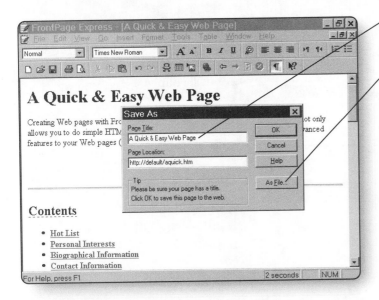

2. Type a **title** for the page in the Page Title text box.

3. **Click** on the **As File button** to save the page to your computer. The Save As File dialog box will open.

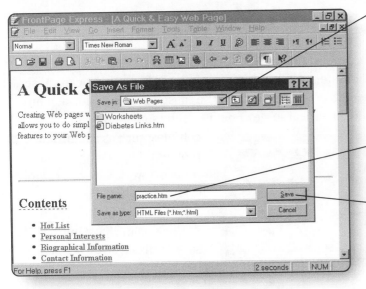

4. **Click** on the **down arrow** next to the Save in list box and **choose** the **directory** in which you want to store the Web page. The directory will appear in the Save in box.

5. Type a **file name** for the Web page in the File name text box.

6. **Click** on **Save**. The Web page will be stored on your computer's hard drive in the directory that you specified.

NOTE

The next time that you click on the Save button, you will not see these dialog boxes. The Web page will automatically be saved to the directory and file name that you previously specified.

VIEWING FRONTPAGE TOOLBARS

Toolbars provide a shortcut to the most often used FrontPage Express functions. Rather than having to search through menus to find the appropriate command, you can use the buttons right in front of you. The graphic on each button will give you a good idea of its function. If you hold the mouse pointer over a toolbar button, a screen tip will appear telling you the function a button performs. But, in favor of seeing more of your Web page, you may not wish to see the toolbars all of the time.

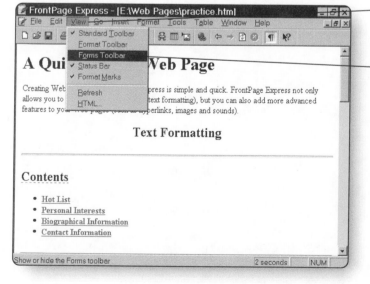

1. **Click** on **View**. The View menu will appear.

2. **Click** on a **toolbar** that is preceded by a check mark. The toolbar will disappear.

3. **Click** on **View**. The View menu will appear.

4. **Click** on a **toolbar** that is not preceded by a check mark. The toolbar will appear.

20 Making Your Web Pages Look Good

Now that you have created the words that will give your Web page meaning, it's time to add some pizzazz. Visitors to your Web site not only look for good content, but they also want to see something that is visually appealing. They'll want to see color and animation. They may also want to listen to a few good tunes. Choose the pictures and sounds for your Web page as carefully as you chose the words. In this chapter, you'll learn how to:

✦ Create hyperlinks to other Web sites

✦ Add backgrounds, images, and sounds to your Web page

✦ Preview your page before you publish it on the Web

CREATING HYPERLINKS

If you have some favorite Web sites that you want to share with visitors to your Web page, make it easy for them by creating a hyperlink. Before you create a hyperlink to another Web site, you should check with the owner of the site and ask permission. You can find information about the owner by looking through the Web site or by sending an e-mail message.

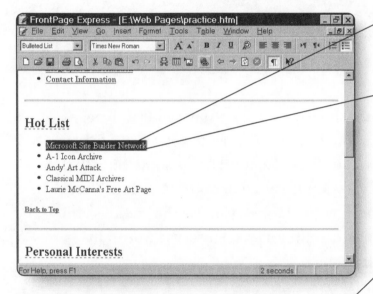

1. Type some **text** to describe the Web page to which you will be linking.

2. Use the mouse to **select** the **words** that will serve as the hyperlink.

3. Click on the **Create or Edit Hyperlink button**. The Create Hyperlink dialog box will open with the World Wide Web tab on top.

4. In the URL text box, **type** the **URL** of the Web page to which you want to link.

5. Click on **OK**.

TIP

You can also create a hyperlink to another page within your own Web site. In the Create Hyperlink dialog box, click on the New Page tab and give the new page a title and file name. You will then have a Web site that contains two pages.

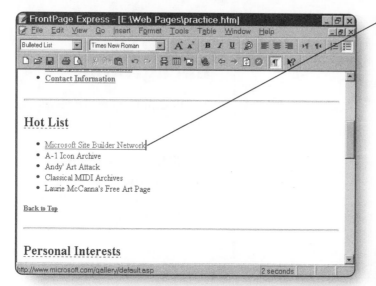

You will be returned to your Web page, and the text that you highlighted will be blue and underlined.

ADDING GRAPHICS AND MULTIMEDIA

Lights, camera, action! Now it's time to show the world what you're made of. This is your chance to show off your artistic talents, or maybe you just want to show off your new goldfish. Whether you create your own images, scan photographs, or use some of the free art found on the Web, it's easy to add these elements to your Web page.

FREE ART ON THE WEB

Here are a few good places on the Web where you can find free pictures, sounds, and other multimedia elements that you can use in your personal Web pages:

Microsoft SiteBuilder Network Gallery at **http://www.microsoft.com/gallery/default.asp**

A-1 Icon Archive at **http://www.free-graphics.com/**

Andy's Art Attack at **http://www.andyart.com/**

A and E MIDI Archives at **http://powerpub.com/aeprod/freemidi.htm**

Laurie McCanna's Free Art Page at **http://www.mccannas.com/free/freeart.htm**

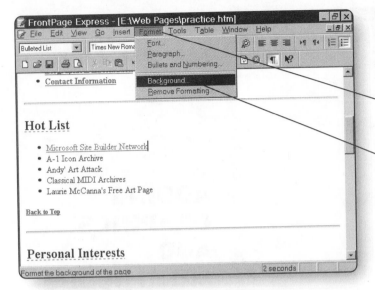

Giving Your Web Page a Background

1. Click on **Format**. The Format menu will appear.

2. Click on **Background**. The Page Properties dialog box will open and the Background tab should be on top.

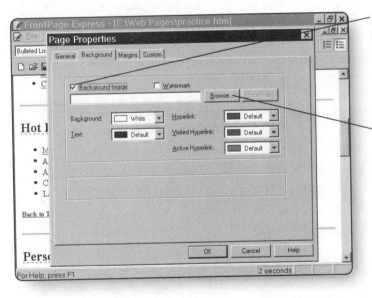

3. Click on the **Background Image checkbox** to add an image as the background. A check mark will be placed in the box.

4. Click on the **Browse button**. The Select Background Image dialog box will appear.

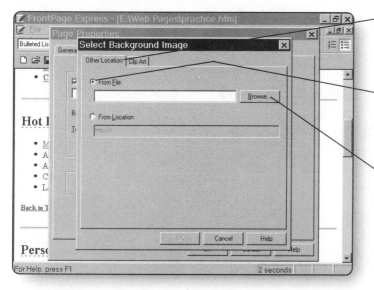

5. **Click** on the **Other Location tab**. The Other Location tab will come to the top of the stack.

6. **Click** on the **From File option button**. The option will be selected.

7. **Click** on the **Browse button**. The Select Background Image dialog box will appear.

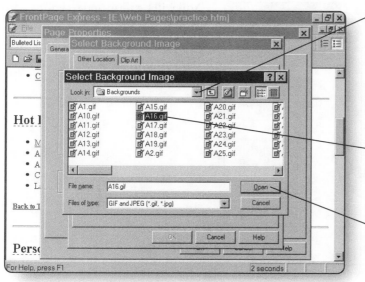

8. **Click** on the **down arrow** next to the Look in list box and **choose** the **directory** in which you have stored graphic images. The directory will appear in the Look in box.

9. **Click** on a **file name** for the background image that you want to use. The file will be selected.

10. **Click** on **Open**. The Page Properties dialog box will appear, and the path and file name of the background image will display in the text box.

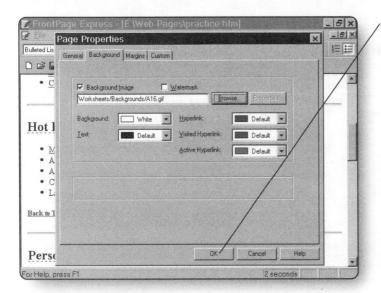

11. Click on OK.

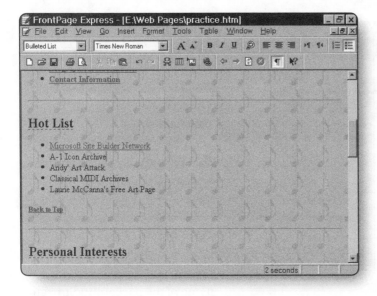

You will be returned to your FrontPage Express Web page and will be able to see how your background looks on the Web page.

Inserting an Image into Your Web Page

1. **Place** the **cursor** in your Web page where you want to insert the image.

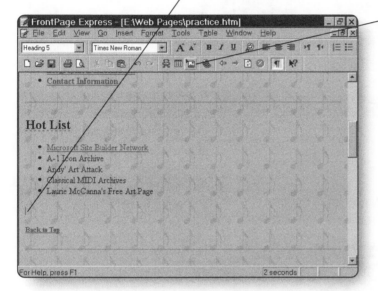

2. **Click** on the **Insert Image button**. The Image dialog box will appear and the Other Location tab should be displayed.

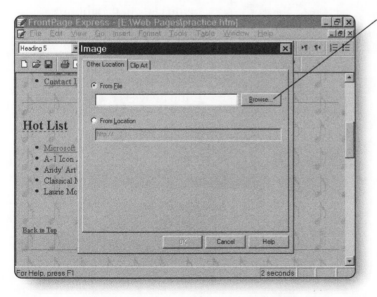

3. **Click** on the **Browse button**. A second Image dialog box will appear.

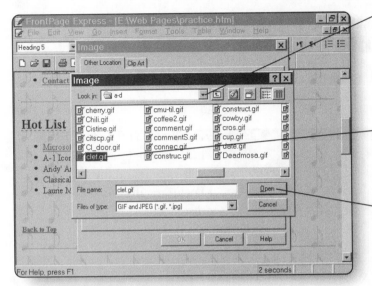

4. Click on the **down arrow** next to the Look in list box and **choose** the **directory** in which you have stored images. The directory will appear in the Look in box.

5. Click on the **file name** for the image that you want to use. The file will be selected.

6. Click on **Open**. The previous Image dialog box will return. The path and file name of the image will display in the From File text box.

7. Click on **OK**.

The image will appear on your Web page.

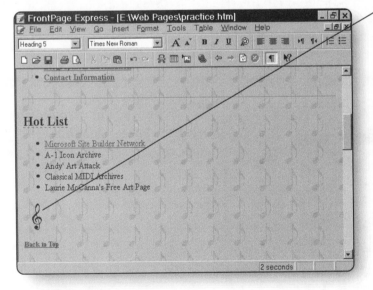

TIP

You can change the size of an image by clicking on it to display the image handles. Then click and drag an image handle until the image is the size you want.

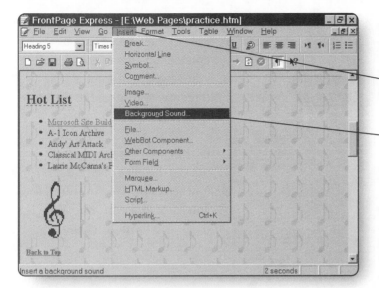

Adding Sound to Your Web Page

1. **Click** on **Insert**. The Insert menu will appear.

2. **Click** on **Background Sound**. The Background Sound dialog box will appear.

TIP

Your safest bet when adding a background sound to your Web page is to use the MIDI format. By using MIDI files, you can be assured that the majority of the people visiting your page will be able to hear your music.

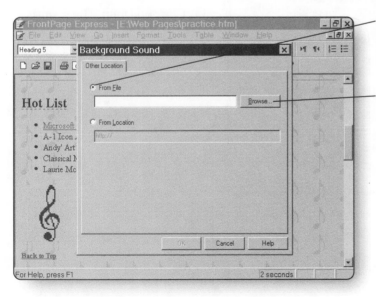

3. **Click** on the **From File option button**. The option will be selected.

4. **Click** on **Browse**. Another Background Sound dialog box will open.

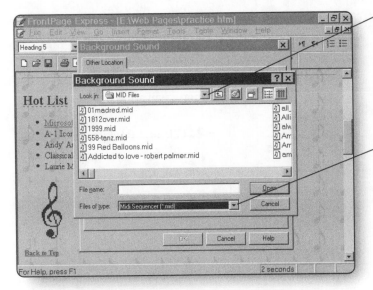

5. Click on the **down arrow** next to the Look in list box and **choose** the **directory** in which you have stored sounds. The directory will appear in the Look in box.

6. Click on the **down arrow** next to the Files of type list box and **select** the **type of sound file** you want to use in your Web page. The file type will be selected.

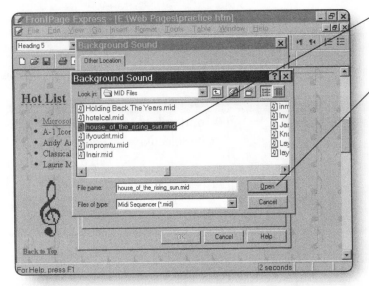

7. Click on the **sound file** that you want to play in your Web page. The file will be selected.

8. Click on **Open**. The sound will be added to your Web page.

PREVIEWING YOUR WEB PAGE

Before you publish your page on the Web, you may want to see what it will look like when viewed in a browser.

1. **Click** on the **Internet Explorer icon** on your desktop. The Internet Explorer browser will open.

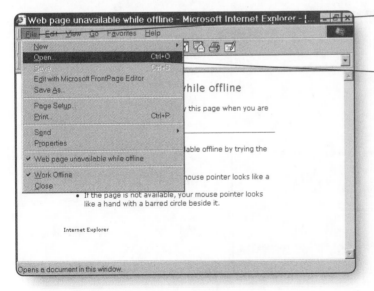

2. **Click** on **File**. The File menu will appear.

3. **Click** on **Open**. The Open dialog box will open.

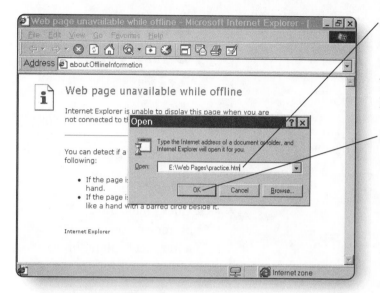

4. In the Open text box, **type the path for the directory and the file name** to specify where your FrontPage Express Web page is stored.

5. Click on OK.

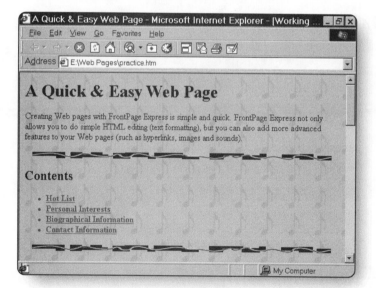

You will be able to see the images and hear the sounds that you added to your Web page.

NOTE

Check with your Internet Service Provider for instructions on how to publish your Web pages.

PART VI REVIEW QUESTIONS

1. What is the fastest and easiest way to start a Web page? *See "Getting Started with Wizards" in Chapter 19.*

2. How do you select text in a Web page for editing? *See "Editing Text" in Chapter 19.*

3. How do you move and copy text? *See "Editing Text" in Chapter 19.*

4. What are the different text formatting commands that can be executed from the Formatting toolbar? *See "Formatting Text" in Chapter 19.*

5. How do you turn toolbars on and off in FrontPage Express? *See "Viewing FrontPage Toolbars" in Chapter 19.*

6. How do you add hyperlinks to your Web page? *See "Creating Hyperlinks" in Chapter 20.*

7. Is it possible to add a new page to your Web and create a hyperlink that points to it? *See "Creating Hyperlinks" in Chapter 20.*

8. How do you add a background to your Web page? *See "Giving Your Web Page a Background" in Chapter 20.*

9. How do you add sound to your Web page so that visitors will hear it when they access your page from the Internet? *See "Adding Sound to Your Web Page" in Chapter 20.*

10. What is the easiest sound format to use in your Web page? *See "Adding Sound to Your Web Page" in Chapter 20.*

Appendix: Installing Internet Explorer

When you install Internet Explorer, you are given three installation options: minimal, standard, or custom installation. This book assumes that you've installed all of the Internet Explorer components. If you did only a minimal or standard installation, you can always return to the Microsoft Web site and download any additional components that you feel will be useful to you. In this appendix, you'll learn how to:

✦ Download Internet Explorer from the Web and install it on your computer

✦ Install additional Internet Explorer components to enhance your Web travels

INSTALLING INTERNET EXPLORER FROM THE WEB

You can always find the latest version of Internet Explorer at the Microsoft Internet Explorer Web site. This section will walk you through the process of downloading the Internet Explorer program files and installing them on your computer.

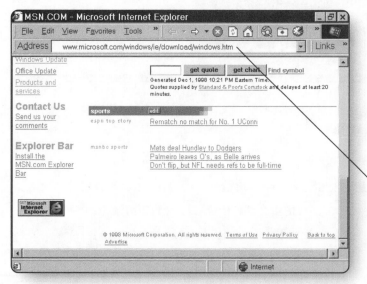

1. **Open** your **Web browser**. You do not have to use Microsoft Internet Explorer to perform the installation; you can use Netscape Navigator or another Web browser. The Web browser will appear on your computer screen.

2. **Click** in the **Address box**, type **www.microsoft.com/ windows/ie/download/ windows.htm**, and **press Enter**. The Internet Explorer Products Download page will appear.

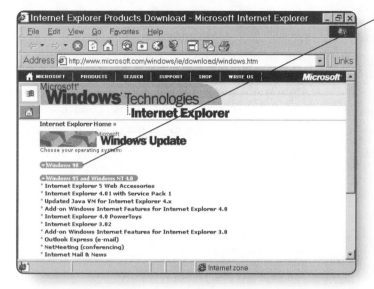

3. Click on the **link** that corresponds to the operating system that you have installed on your computer. The list will expand to display the Internet Explorer components available for that operating system.

4. Click on the **Internet Explorer 5.0 link**. The Internet Explorer page will appear.

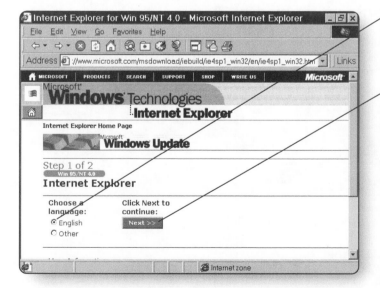

5. Click on a **language option button**. The option will be selected.

6. Click on **Next**. Step 2 of the download process will display in the browser window.

7. Click on an **option button** that corresponds to a Web site that is located closest to you. The option will be selected.

8. Click on **Next**. The File Download dialog box will open.

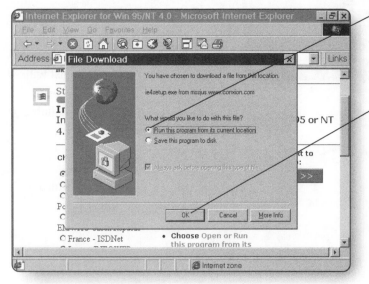

9. Click on the **Run this program from its current location** option button. The option will be selected.

10. Click on **OK**. The File Download dialog box will open.

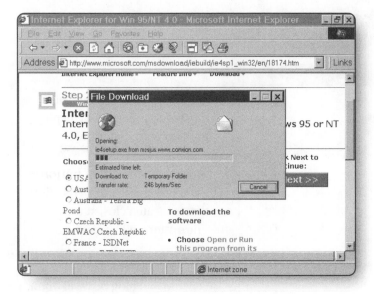

11. Wait while the file downloads to your computer. When the download is finished, a Security Warning dialog box will open.

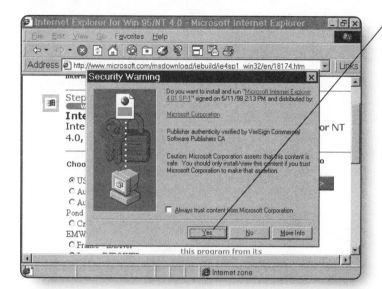

12. **Click** on **Yes**. The Setup Wizard will start.

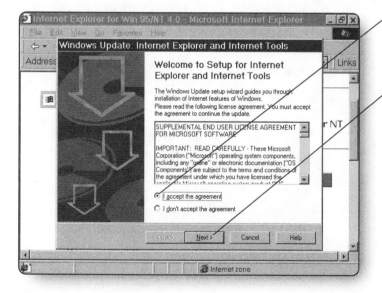

13. **Click** on the **I accept the agreement option button**. The option will be selected.

14. **Click** on **Next**. The Install page of the wizard will appear.

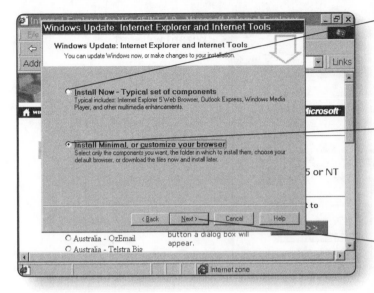

15a. Click on the **Install Now option button** if you want to use the easiest installation method. The option will be selected.

OR

15b. Click on the **Install Minimal option button** if you want to customize the installation. The option will be selected.

16. Click on **Next**. The Component Options page will appear.

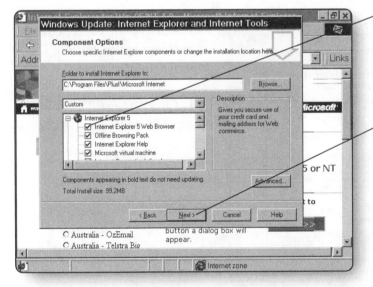

17. Click in **the checkbox** next to those software products that you want installed on your computer. A check mark will appear in the box.

18. Click on **Next**. You will be asked to select from a number of download sites.

19. Click on the **site** located closest to you. The download site will be selected.

20. Click on **Next**. The download will begin and a progress dialog box will open.

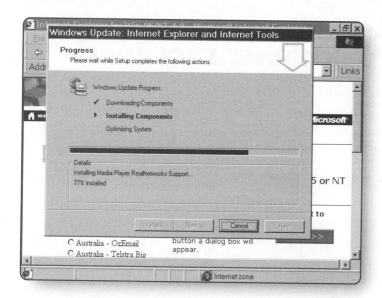

21. Wait while the software downloads and begins the installation process.

The Details area will tell you approximately how much time will be needed for the download, and then the progress of the installation. When the installation is complete, the Restart Computer page will appear.

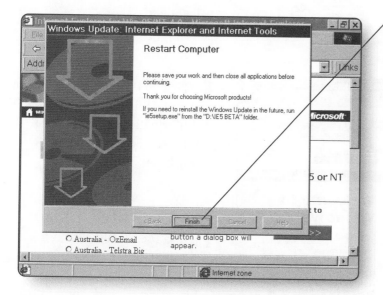

22. Click on **Finish**. Your computer will restart and will update your computer systems setting to run Internet Explorer. This may take a while.

ADDING COMPONENTS TO INTERNET EXPLORER

The number of additional software components available to you is vast. These are what give Internet Explorer its power. Some components add functionality to the browser, such as the VRML viewer, sound packs, and multimedia. Other components take you beyond the basic browser and into the world of electronic mail, Chat, and video conferencing.

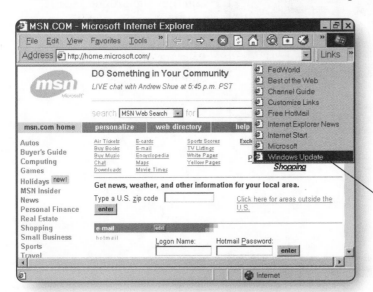

1. **Open** the Internet Explorer **browser**. The browser will appear on your computer screen.

2. **Click** on the **Windows Update button** on the Links bar. The Windows Update Web page will appear.

3. **Click** on **Product Updates** and wait while the setup gathers the information it needs to continue. A Security Warning dialog box will open.

NOTE

This process may take several minutes.

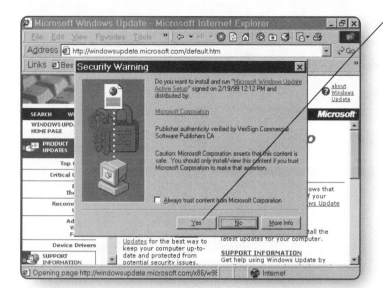

4. Click on **Yes**. A confirmation dialog box will open.

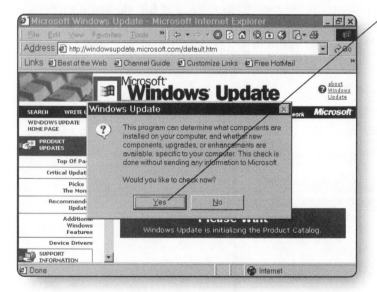

5. Click on **Yes**. The setup will look through your computer and determine which Internet Explorer components are already installed. A list of components available will appear.

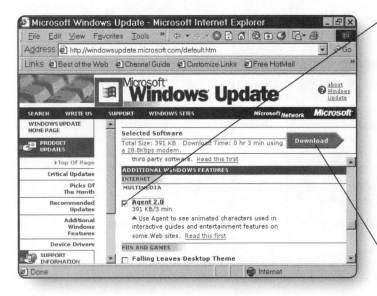

6. Click in the **check box** next to each component that you want to install on your computer. A check will appear in the box.

> **TIP**
>
> Click the arrow next to the component name for a description of that component.

7. Click on **Download**. The Download Checklist page will appear.

> **NOTE**
>
> Look at the Selected Software box at the top of the page to see an estimate of how long it will take to install the selected components.

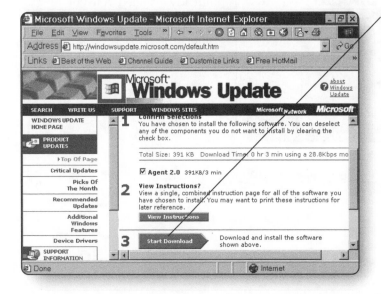

8. Click on **Start Download**. The Software License Agreement dialog box will open.

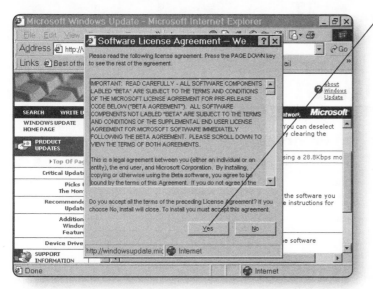

9. **Click** on **Yes**. The Windows Update status dialog box will open.

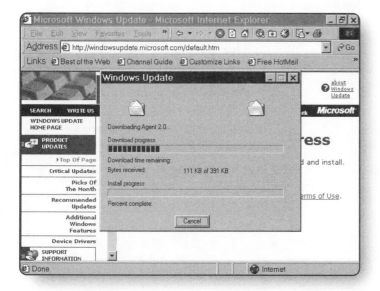

10. Wait while the component downloads to your computer. After the required installation files have downloaded to your computer, the program will begin the installation process. When this is complete, a confirmation dialog box will appear.

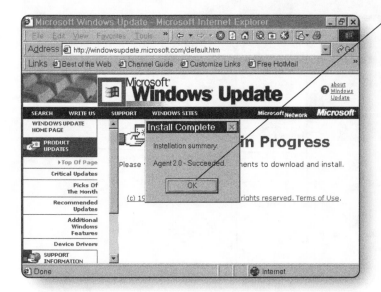

11. Click on OK. The components you selected are now installed on your computer and ready to perform their Web functions.

Glossary

3-D. A visual effect that makes images appear to have depth.

Address bar. An area where you can type the URL address of the Web page you want to access. With AutoComplete, it isn't always necessary to type the entire URL address; the browser can do some of that for you. You can also perform searches from the address bar.

Animated GIF. A type of GIF graphic that combines several images into a single file. When the animated GIF file is viewed, the images display in a continuous cycle, as if you were watching a cartoon. GIF animation doesn't give the same level of control and flexibility as other animation formats. It is popular because animated GIFs can be viewed in any Web browser, and the GIF file size is typically small.

Anonymous FTP. A file transfer method that allows users to access a server without the need of a password. Usually, you would log in as anonymous and use your e-mail address as a password.

Applet. A small Java program that runs in a Web page. Java applets can take a long time to download to your computer.

AU. Audio. The most common file format for transmitting sound over the Internet. If you want to play .au files that you find on the Internet, you will need a special audio player, such as Microsoft Media Player or Real Networks RealPlayer.

Authentication. The process of identifying an individual, usually based on a username and password. Authentication merely ensures that the individual is who he or she claims to be, but says nothing about the access rights of the individual.

AutoComplete. A feature used in the Address bar that suggests possible URL addresses based on the text you are typing.

AutoSearch. A feature used in the Address bar that performs a search based on words you provide. Type **go**, **find**, or **?**, type a search word, and press Enter.

Browser. A software program needed to navigate Web pages and FTP sites on the Internet.

Business Card. The entry in the Windows Address Book that contains your contact information. A Business Card entry contains your name and e-mail address. You can also add your home address and phone number, the URL address for your personal Web page, your business address and phone number, and the URL address for your business.

Cable modem. A modem that operates over cable TV lines. Cable TV lines have a greater bandwidth than telephone lines and allow for faster access to the Internet. This is new technology that is still developing. There are a couple of hurdles that need to be overcome before cable modem connections to the Internet are widely available.

Carpal tunnel syndrome. A common occupational hazard for intense Web surfers. Carpal tunnel syndrome occurs when the same small finger or wrist movements are repeated over and over.

Certificate Authority. A trusted third-party organization or company that issues digital certificates used to create digital signatures and public-private key pairs. The role of the Certificate Authority is to guarantee that the individual granted the certificate is, in fact, who he or she claims to be.

Channels. Web sites that are automatically updated and downloaded to your computer on a schedule specified by the channel content provider.

Compression. A method of squeezing a file so that it fits into a smaller size. Compressed files transfer much more quickly.

Content Advisor. A feature of Internet Explorer and its components that gives you control over the type of content that your computer can access on the Internet. By using the Content Advisor, you can set up your Internet Explorer suite programs so that Web sites, newsgroups, and Chat rooms that are offensive to you cannot be accessed from your computer.

Cookie. A piece of information that a Web server stores on your computer until it's time for the server to read it. For example, a cookie that is made while you shop around a Web mall contains a list of the items you're planning to purchase. This way you can leave the Web site and your list of items will be saved so that you can resume your shopping spree next time you return to the mall.

Cross-posting. The practice of posting a message to more than one newsgroup. This is only proper netiquette if the topic is of interest to more than one newsgroup.

Dial-up. A type of Internet connection established when you dial a number through your computer's modem to connect to your ISP.

Digital certificate. An attachment to an e-mail message used to keep the contents of the message secure. Digital certificates are used to verify that users sending messages are who they claim to be, and to provide the receiver with the means to encode a reply. An individual wishing to send an encrypted message applies for a digital certificate from a Certificate Authority. The Certificate Authority issues an encrypted digital certificate containing the applicant's public key. The recipient of the encrypted message uses the Certificate Authority's public key to decode the digital certificate attached to the message.

Digitizing tablet. An electronic board that detects the movement of a pen or a cursor, enabling you to enter drawings and sketches into a computer. The cursor is similar to a mouse except that it has a window with crosshairs for pinpoint placement and has as many as 16 buttons. A digitizing pen looks like a ballpoint pen but uses an electronic head instead of ink. Most digitizing tablets support a mouse emulation mode where the pen or cursor acts like a mouse.

Directory services. Search tools you can use to find the e-mail and postal addresses for individuals and businesses. There are several directory services that you can access from the Windows Address Book.

Dynamic HTML. A programming language that creates interactive Web pages that do not require long transfer times between your computer and the server. Dynamic HTML can change the way elements look without refreshing the browser window, change the objects that appear in the browser window without having to access the server for the object, animate objects on a Web page, and build interactive forms.

E-mail. Electronic mail. Electronic correspondence system where messages are sent over a network such as the Internet.

Explorer bar. A feature in Internet Explorer that enables you to see your list of favorites, search results, or history in a frame within the browser window while still allowing you to view Web pages.

FAQ. Frequently Asked Questions. A list of responses on a particular subject that answers questions most often asked by new users. Before asking questions in a newsgroup, read the newsgroup's FAQ and see if your question has already been answered.

Favorite. A URL address stored in the Internet Explorer browser that can be accessed easily from the Favorites menu or the Favorites button. You can add more than just Web sites to your list of Favorites; you can also add newsgroups and Chat rooms.

Flame. To send a message that is hostile, rude, or that in some way displays inappropriate behavior.

Form. A method used in Web pages to collect data from visitors to the Web site.

Frame. A method of dividing the browser display area into separate sections, each of which is really a different Web page.

FTP. File Transfer Protocol. A method of sending and receiving computer files over the Internet.

Full-duplex. The transmission of data in two directions simultaneously. When you talk on the telephone, you are using a full-duplex device because both parties can talk at the same time. When using full-duplex, the data that is transmitted does not appear on your screen until it has been received and a confirmation has been sent back by the other party. This ensures that the data has been transmitted correctly.

GIF. Graphics Interchange Format. A file format that compresses computer-generated images in order to prepare them for viewing in Web pages.

Half-duplex. The transmission of data in one direction at a time. When using half-duplex, each character that is transmitted appears immediately on your screen. This is called local echo because the characters are echoed by the local device.

History list. A list of all the URLs that were visited during past Internet sessions. You can use the History list to return to a page you visited previously during an Internet session. You can change the number of days that a URL is kept in your History list.

HTML. Hypertext Markup Language. One of the common languages used to create Web pages.

Hyperlink. Text, usually underlined and often displayed in a different color, that you can click on to access another Web page or an FTP server.

Hypermedia. The use of hypertext, images, sound, video, animation, and other media in a Web page.

Image map. A graphical image that has several hyperlinks contained in it.

Inbox Assistant. Manages your incoming e-mail. The Inbox Assistant can automatically sort messages into folders, forward messages to people you specify, or delete messages that you don't want to see.

Internet. A global computer network where users can share files, exchange e-mail, converse in newsgroups, and view Web pages.

ISP. Internet Service Provider. A company that provides Internet access for its customers.

JPEG. Joint Photographic Experts' Group. A file format that compresses photographic images in order to prepare them for viewing in Web pages.

Jump. To move from one Web page to another using hyperlinks.

Lurker. A person who reads newsgroup postings, but who rarely joins the discussion. When you visit a newsgroup for the first time, you are encouraged to lurk until you have a feel for how the newsgroup operates.

Marquee. Information that scrolls across the screen in a Web page.

MIDI. Musical Instrument Digital Interface. A file format used to store music.

MIME. Multipurpose Internet Mail Extension. A method for sending non-textual data, such as audio files and graphic images, in encoded attachments to e-mail messages.

MPEG. Motion Picture Experts Group. A file format for high-quality video compression.

Netiquette. Techie-speak for Internet etiquette. This is the informal code of manners that governs online conduct.

Newsgroup. A discussion forum on the Internet.

Newsgroup filters. These filters allow you to specify the types of newsgroup messages that you do not want to view. The filter prevents the message from being downloaded to your computer and from displaying the header information in the list of messages.

Noise. Interference in the telephone line that destroys the integrity of data signals. Noise comes from a variety of sources such as radio waves, electrical wires, lightning, and bad connections. One of the advantages of fiber optic cable is that it is much less susceptible to noise.

Offline browsing. Being able to view Web pages without being connected to your ISP or the Internet. You can use offline browsing if you don't want to tie up the phone line or if you don't have access to the Internet. You must download Web pages to your computer before you can view them offline.

Online Session. The time you spend on the Internet. The session begins when you connect to your ISP; it includes everything you do, from lurking through newsgroups to downloading files from an FTP server, and ends when you hang up.

Personal certificate. This stores information about you, usually a name and password, and it is used when you access a site that needs verification of your identity.

Postmaster. The person who makes sure that the electronic mail always gets delivered for a given domain. The postmaster also handles complaints against mail accounts within that domain. If someone is using the Internet inappropriately, send an e-mail to postmaster@domain.com, substituting the relevant domain name into the e-mail address.

Profile Assistant. Stores personal information that you have supplied and allows you to share this information with Web sites that need it. You don't have to re-type this information every time you visit a Web site. Others cannot use this information without your permission.

Protocol. A set of rules and standards that allows computers to transfer information.

Restricted Sites zone. A security zone that contains sites from which you do not want to download files because you feel that the downloaded content could damage your computer.

Screen Tip. A Windows Help feature that displays a flag description onscreen when the mouse is held over a screen element.

Scrollbar. A Windows screen element that is used in conjunction with the mouse to move to different areas of a page.

Search engine. A program that searches through a database. When you request information on a subject, the search engine returns a list of possible matches.

Security certificate. A file on your computer that is used as your identification for Internet commerce.

Security zones. A feature in Internet Explorer that allows you to specify the type of content that can be downloaded to your computer based on the zone into which the Web site falls.

Start Page. The Web page that first appears when you open the Internet Explorer browser. You can set the start page to be any page that you want. It can be a page from a Web site you visit often, a blank page, or a page that is stored on your computer's hard drive.

Stationery. A feature of Outlook Express that makes creating HTML messages a snap. There are several stationery styles installed with Outlook Express. Each style contains a background that sets the theme and a text style that complements the background. You can design your own stationery to use in Outlook Express.

Streaming. A technique for transferring data so that it can be processed as a steady and continuous stream. Streaming technologies are becoming increasingly important with the growth of the Internet because most users do not have fast enough access to download large multimedia files quickly. With streaming, the client browser or plug-in can start displaying the data before the entire file has been transmitted.

Subscription. Allows you to set a schedule by which the Internet Explorer browser will automatically check to see if a Web site has been updated.

TCP/IP. Transmission Control Protocol/Internet Protocol. The predominant method used to manage communication over the Internet.

Telecommuting. Jack Nilles first used this term in the early 1970s to describe a work environment where workers can work at home and transmit data and documents to a central office via telephone lines.

Text mode. A browser view that displays text only. You cannot view graphic images, VRML, or sound while in text mode.

Thread. The list of replies to an e-mail or newsgroup message. Threads allow you to follow the flow of messages in a conversation topic. As you read through a thread, you will read messages in the order of their posting to the newsgroup and in the context of the messages to which they were responding.

Trusted Sites zone. A security zone that contains sites from which you believe you can download files without worrying about potentially damaging content.

URL. Uniform Resource Locator. A standardized method of identifying a Web page on the Internet. URLs consist of a service, the domain, and a directory path.

Usenet. An Internet service that provides approximately 20,000 discussion forums that are open to the Internet public.

Videoconferencing. Using a computer network to transmit audio and video data when conducting a conference between two or more people located at different sites. Each person has a video camera, microphone, and speakers attached to his or her computer. Voices, video, and data are carried over the network and are delivered to the other conference participants.

Virtual reality. An artificial environment created with computer hardware and software. The virtual reality environment simulates a real environment. To "enter" a virtual reality, you wear special gloves, earphones, and goggles which receive their input from the computer system. In addition to feeding sensory input to you, the devices also monitor your actions. The goggles track your eye movements and respond accordingly by sending new video input.

VRML. Virtual Reality Modeling Language. A World Wide Web specification for displaying 3-dimensional objects. VRML produces a 3-dimensional space that appears onscreen. You can move within this space by pressing keys to turn left or right, up or down, or to go forward or backward. The images change, giving you the impression that you are moving through real space. To view VRML files, you need a VRML browser or a VRML plug-in to a Web browser.

Web site certificate. This guarantees the identity of a secure Web site, making sure that no other Web site assumes its identity.

Webcasting. Using the World Wide Web to broadcast information. Unlike typical surfing, which relies on a pull method of transferring Web pages, Webcasting uses push technologies. One of the first Webcasting services was PointCast.

Webmaster. The person responsible for maintaining a Web site.

World Wide Web. A system of hypertext documents (Web pages) that can be accessed over the Internet.

Index

T

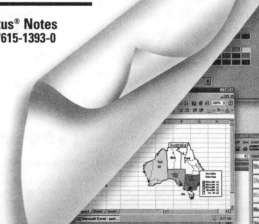